Billion Dollar Lies

How Lennar Corporation Swindled Pensioners, Lenders, And Partners And Undermined The Foundation Of Our Justice System

by Nicolas Marsch

Swan Mountain Press
2014

Published by:
Swan Mountain Press
New York City, NY
www.billiondollarlies.com

Copyright 2014, Nicolas Marsch

ISBN 13 digit: 978-0-9862448-0-3

Library of Congress Cataloging-in-Publication Data
Swan Mountain Press/Marsch, Nicolas

p. cm

Cover art by Swan Mountain Press

FIRST EDITION

Billion Dollar Lies

How Lennar Corporation Swindled Pensioners, Lenders, And Partners And Undermined The Foundation Of Our Justice System

TABLE OF CONTENTS

We are not a reactive company. We are anticipatory in our approach to almost anything . . . we try to do things strategically and by plan. — Stuart Miller, CEO Lennar Corp.

INTRODUCTION

THIS BOOK IS about Lennar Corporation and its key executives. Lennar is a NYSE-listed homebuilder headquartered in Miami, Florida. The book exposes their unique way of doing business, an approach that can best be described as the Lennar Way. As this story unfolds, you will learn what the "Lennar Way" means, and importantly, what it signifies to those who have had the misfortune of doing business with this company.

Lennar was unexpectedly "Under New Management" when the company's co-founder, Leonard Miller, suddenly stepped down as CEO in 1997 due to illness and his son Stuart was appointed to take his place.

As one goes about daily life you often see an Under New Management banner on a business. Generally the act of posting such a banner is essentially proclaiming that customers can expect a better product and a better experience. Not in Lennar's case.

Few companies, listed or otherwise, have gone through a transformation quite like Lennar under Stuart Miller's "guidance" and "direction." And it certainly wasn't to give those with whom they do business a better product and a better experience.

Close examination of Lennar's business practices from 1997 forward reveals that, under new management, Lennar has left a chilling trail of broken promises, dishonored agreements, ruined ventures, unpaid loans, and defrauded partners across our country. And it is a pattern that repeats over and over no matter where or with whom they do business. It's always the same.

And, unfortunately, this company and its executives appear to be emblematic of what is wrong with much of corporate America today. Only in the rarest of instances does the maxim—"Commit the crime, Do the time" apply to these modern day robber barons. They maraud and defraud on a grand scale with little or no consequence. And the worst that can happen — if they get caught — is that the company (meaning the shareholders) pays a fine — tax deductible — just an additional cost of doing business.

Our financial system was nearly destroyed recently by rampant and pervasive mortgage fraud. Credit markets imploded and the effects of these egregious actions are still felt to this day. Fines were paid, but almost no one went to jail as a result. Why is that?

Here you will meet some of the most crooked executives operating in America (at least since Enron went out of business and its top executives, including CEO Jeffrey Skilling, went to prison). And speaking of Enron, there are a number of astonishing parallels between this Lennar story and Enron that will surprise you.

You will also see and learn just how corporate fraud and deception work at the highest levels. We aren't talking about low or mid-level rogue executives, either, although there are certainly a few of those in our story. And you will be able to observe how, with enough money and an army of slick lawyers, our legal system can routinely be manipulated, subverted, and used to actually enrich companies like Lennar, and corporate executives like Stuart Miller.

All it takes is money — a lot of it — to accomplish things in our legal system that would be unimaginable to the average citizen. And if the system is vulnerable to their tactics, then so are those who depend on our rule of law to go about their daily lives.

This book has been researched and written primarily using sworn testimony and documents obtained from Lennar Corporation itself, its executives, news accounts, and other sources. Documents are readily available on this book's website www.billiondollarlies.com. Whenever possible, their own clear, concise, and in-context sworn testimony is quoted verbatim. Objections made by legions of Lennar lawyers have been omitted from their testimony to achieve clarity and brevity.

There is the use of clearly identified hypothetical dialog or a hypothetical meeting sketched out here and there to illustrate a point. News accounts are introduced at various times to identify and direct the reader to additional sources of information.

This book details my personal experiences with Lennar, while also looking across the country and documenting the trail of broken promises, stolen money, and ruined ventures left by these marauders that proves the point that they are a financial crime in progress.

History can't be written contemporaneously. The process of writing this book has benefited immensely from a careful look-back at testimony by top Lennar executives, at key events and actions initiated by them, and a broader look across the country at the strikingly similar pattern of fraud and deceit that is the hallmark of this company. A timeline of key events is included at the end of this book.

You will be presented with numerous "binary" choices as you read this book: True or False? And that means comparing the Lennar executives' sworn testimony to statements made by others whose credibility is unassailable and contrasting statements made by Lennar executives and their lawyers to facts that are undeniable. And there are many instances where statements made by the Lennar executives concerning the same exact topics disagree so much with each other that one (or more) simply have to be lying. You decide.

Lennar's executives and their lawyers have elevated lying to an art form. It is all part of the Lennar Way. A remarkable book by Pulitzer Prize-winning author James B. Stewart titled *Tangled Web* examines the epidemic of lying in this country. His conclusion is that pervasive lying is undermining the foundations of our society. His observations and conclusions could not be more on point to the facts incorporated within this book.

To accomplish their nefarious goals, Lennar and its lawyers routinely employ — in a phrase often attributed to

Lenin—"Useful Idiots." These range from certain media people and outlets, aligned business organizations, and others. Unfortunately, even judges have succumbed to their machinations.

The supreme irony is that the Lennar executives fly the banner of honesty and loudly trumpet their integrity to anyone willing to listen. They engrave it on mirrors distributed to the unsuspecting. "We have integrity" is on their stationary, their business cards, and their website. Read the book and decide for yourself just how much "integrity" this company and its executives really have.

But it has been proven time after time that, with persistence and patience, the truth will come out. It always does. And it is time to get the unfiltered truth out in regard to this company. Thus this book.

There may not be a better example of this concept than Lance Armstrong and his successful intimidation and litigation tactics regarding those who would dare question his "integrity" or alleged use of banned substances. This technique succeeded for years, but how did that eventually turn out?

Lennar is not a household name, and this book may not be of interest to the general public. But it should be of vital interest to those who have had dealings with this company or are considering doing business with them. If you are in the California Public Employees Retirement System (CALPERS), a California taxpayer or United States taxpayer, an investor in a mortgage fund, a Lennar joint venture partner or prospective partner, a lender, supplier, contractor, subcontractor, a former, current, or prospective employee, a Lennar homebuyer or prospective home-buyer, then you should read this book.

If you are already involved with them and have experienced their uniquely crooked way of doing business, you will learn you are not alone. If you have a story about Lennar, its lawyers, its business tactics, and its litigation tactics, let's talk. If you are considering involvement with them, at least you can make an informed decision.

CHAPTER ONE

An Interesting Day

LENNAR CEO STUART Miller had a problem. On January 9, 2009, an investigative company called FDI published a Red Flags Report concerning Lennar Corporation and certain officers of the company, including Miller and his trusted lieutenant Jon Jaffe. The report was highly critical of the business practices and ethical conduct of the company and its key officers.

Negative reports are often published about the company, usually for a good reason, and generally without a response. But in this case Miller was dressed up and whisked off within hours of publication to a remote CNBC studio to be interviewed by correspondent Diane Olick and respond to the allegations in the FDI report.

Three days later Lennar Corporation issued a detailed press release denouncing the Red Flags Report and described the ten Red Flags in the report as *"false statements"*, *"false and scurrilous allegations"* and *"false information."* All ten of them.

Fortunately, video tapes and transcripts of Miller's CNBC interview by Diane Olick, the FDI report, and the Lennar January 12, 2009, press release are available and can be dissected with the benefit of an informed look-back. And a look-back that incorporates subsequent events only further corroborates and validates the main points in the FDI report.

There was nothing *"false"* or *"scurrilous"* about the FDI report, and its ten Red Flags. But its publication and its contents caused Miller and Lennar to engage in a frenzied denial of the validity of each of the reports' Red Flags, and to unleash at least four law firms to pursue, silence, and punish those involved in its publication.

Lennar's claims included "losses" attributed to a decline in Lennar's share price as a result of publication of the report, and "stock manipulation."

Why the claims? Negative reports are published all of the time about Lennar, and they don't sue the authors and publishers no matter how negative the report or article may be, or what impact such a report may have on the stock price.

In fact, on January 8, 2009, just one day before publication of the FDI report, J.P. Morgan issued their own report on Lennar. The J.P. Morgan report was an analysis of Lennar's current financial condition, future prospects, and also their opaque off-balance sheet joint ventures and unquantifiable exposure. This murky off balance sheet activity had always troubled Wall Street and many investors stayed away from Lennar, dubbing it a "black box." A "black box" in Wall St. parlance is a company with an undecipherable balance sheet that may be fraught with un-known and undisclosed risks. Think Enron.

J.P. Morgan questioned the current valuation of the company's share price and called for a significantly lower share price based on their analysis of Lennar's shrinking balance sheet, continuing quarterly and annual losses, and unknown off-balance sheet exposure.

It is worth noting that the FDI report made no men-tion of the Lennar stock price, unlike the J.P. Morgan re-port. In fact, the over-priced Lennar stock *was* the focus of the J.P. Morgan report.

Clearly, prestigious J.P. Morgan is a far more recogniz-able name in the investing world than little FDI. Lennar stock declined the day after the J.P. Morgan report and the day of publication of the FDI report. There was no ap-parent response and no lawsuit filed by Lennar against J.P. Morgan regarding their report and a subsequent decline in the price of Lennar's stock, even though the recom-mended share price by J.P. Morgan was actually about the same as the alleged share price decline Lennar attributed to the FDI report.

The Lennar stock price on the J.P. Morgan publication date of January 8, 2009 was $11.42. The quoted price tar-get in the J.P. Morgan report was $8.50. In fact, less than six weeks earlier, on November 21, 2008, the Lennar stock price was only $3.64. This is about the same price, or less, than a happy meal at McDonalds. And that price is just about three and a half bucks from zero.

So what was it about the FDI report that got Miller's and Lennar's undivided attention?

CHAPTER TWO

The Lennar Way

A LOOK-BACK to January 2009 reveals that the FDI report put an unwelcome and untimely spotlight on Lennar's unsavory business practices.

Lennar's CFO Bruce Gross admitted in testimony on December 2, 2013 that at the point in time when the FDI Red Flags Report was issued Lennar was "extremely vulnerable."

The last thing Stuart Miller wanted to do was appear on CNBC and answer pointed questions generated by the Red Flags Report. But he didn't have a choice. As the FDI report pointed out, Lennar had recently been implicated in a massive swindle of the California Employees Retirement System (CALPERS). This transaction and its aftermath is explained in detail in Chapter 8 of this book.

A key Red Flag in the FDI report recounted that in 2007 Lennar pulled off a remarkable and audacious fraud concerning CALPERS and a Barclay's Bank loan syndicate. CALPERS had been inveigled into contributing assets to a Lennar managed and controlled company — LandSource LLC. Lennar then used CALPERS assets in part to secure a large loan to LandSource funded by a Barclays Bank loan syndicate. The loan closed and funded on March 1, 2007, just as the California and national real estate markets were going off of a cliff.

Lennar then immediately paid itself and LNR, a sister company, a "special dividend" equal to the entire principal balance of the loan, a whopping 1.4 billion dollars, thereby dooming LandSource LLC to an inevitable collapse and bankruptcy just fourteen months later. Further, Lennar reported a gain of over $175,000,000 on the LandSource LLC transaction in the third quarter of 2007.

And in that transaction, CALPERS was clearly defrauded and lost every dollar in real property assets and cash entrusted to Lennar. $922,000,000. Pension money belonging to 1.6 million current and former employees of the State of California. And others lost as well, including over 5,000 unsecured creditors of LandSource.

Stuart Miller lied directly to CNBC correspondent Diane Olick about the validity of many elements of the report, and particularly the CALPERS swindle, claiming that "*All venture partners have lost*", and "*have lost.*" Not true.

CALPERS WASN'T ALONE. Here is a direct quote from an article in the *Fort Myers News-Press*, August 21, 2013 edition, regarding a typical Lennar fraud executed just months before the LandSource swindle:

"The FDIC claims in a lawsuit that

*national builder Lennar Homes —
faced with a collapsing housing market
in 2006 — defrauded lenders by getting straw buyers to overpay for 66
units in the Terraces of Riverwalk con-
dominium.*

*Lennar officials faked records to get
appraisers and lenders to think that a
majority of the units already sold in
Riverwalk were owner occupied, and
that they were much more valuable
than they actually were."*

As our story unfolds, you will see that this little
Lennar caper in Ft. Myers in 2006 was just an off-Broad-
way rehearsal for the aforementioned CALPERS fraud
which has the distinction of being perhaps the biggest
real estate fraud in California history. These are bad actors, indeed.

This typical Lennar conduct is referred to in this book
as the Lennar Way. The Lennar Way is a series of unsavory
and dishonest practices that include gaming and abusing
the trust of lenders, partners, suppliers, employees, contractors, subcontractors, joint venture participants, and
homebuyers.

There is a hidden agenda in place at the inception of
every relationship initiated by Lennar. Once they ooze their
way into control of the checkbook and gain access to the
cash and valuable assets of others, it is game, set, match,
and Lennar wins every time. Remember, they plan ahead.

Arrogance and greed rule the day at this company. And an utter disregard for other people's money. Written agreements and the rule of law mean nothing to the Lennar executives, as you will see.

Hundreds of lawsuits and complaints have been filed across the country by hapless victims that recount the horrors of doing business with these people. Highlights (or lowlights) from some of these complaints are detailed in Chapter 19 of this book.

Complaints have also been filed in multiple states with Attorneys General over their business practices. Lennar has periodically been under investigation by the SEC and the FBI. Newspapers routinely recount their fraudulent activities across the country.

And nobody is off limits to them. Nobody. Not pensioners, not partners, not lenders, not home buyers, not employees, and not even the U.S. Government.

The FDI Red Flags Report allegations included fraud, money laundering, and the aforementioned swindling of CALPERS and Barclay's Bank. The report also, among other things, questioned the adequacy of disclosures of key information in the company's quarterly and annual reports.

It was imperative that Lennar bury the report, and they set out to accomplish this by overwhelming and killing the messengers. In response to the report, Lennar and its lawyers concocted huge damage claims and filed a lawsuit in hometown Miami, Florida. And what better place to "bury" it than in Lennar's backyard?

Since filing their Miami lawsuit, Lennar has squandered tens of millions of dollars of shareholder money pursuing their fabricated damage claims, thereby engaging in yet another massive multilayered fraud, this time on the U.S. Court System and the U.S. Attorney's office in Miami.

Lennar's Miami damage claims based on share price decline allegedly attributable to the FDI publication were and are ridiculous and fraudulent. A Florida Fairy Tale, as outlined in Chapter 17.

It is a fact that Lennar's stock price has always been historically volatile. News reports critical of Lennar's business tactics and substandard reporting in their quarterly and annual reports surface all the time. Analysts are often critical as well. That comes with the territory when you are running a company primarily to benefit a few key executives and Stuart Miller's personal friends. But Lennar doesn't generally sue the publishers, reporters, or analysts because it would draw unwanted attention to their unique way of doing business. And when Lennar chooses a litigation target, size matters. They couldn't intimidate or overwhelm J.P. Morgan, but FDI was another story.

CHAPTER THREE

Under New Management

STUART MILLER'S SUDDEN and unanticipated appointment to CEO in 1997 occurred at exactly the same time the ink was drying on a development deal I made with Lennar on a large residential and golf project in California called the Bridges at Rancho Santa Fe. I had done due diligence on Lennar. There was nothing alarming uncovered in that process. No litigation outside of normal "comes with the territory" home defect lawsuits. No partner disputes, no lender lawsuits, no fraud claims, and no breach of contract claims either. Clean bill of health.

This may have been the worst timing in the history of timing. Unbeknownst to me at the time, Stuart Miller was an apple that had fallen very, very far from the tree. He had been standing in his father's shadow — just biding his time — and waiting for his chance to seize control of the company.

Let's go back and see how this relationship got started.

CHAPTER FOUR

The Beginning

I HAD INTERESTS in a spectacular parcel of land located in Rancho Santa Fe, California, just north of San Diego. This upscale rural community is often ranked among the top places to live in the United States. And maybe the world. The site was incredible: deep canyons, flowing water, rolling hills, orange groves, and a perfect climate.

In 1985 our development team implemented the design of a world-class golf and residential community on the land and obtained building permits in record time. This was because I had long-standing relationships with key community members and the San Diego County Board of Supervisors.

This project is now called the Bridges at Rancho Santa Fe, and is colloquially referred to as the Bridges. The development plan for my project was simple and straight-forward: design and build the best golf course in California. Nothing less. I retained Robert Trent Jones II

and his talented design team and they undertook the daunting golf course design process. Daunting because of the
unique terrain we had to work with to lay out the course.

It was a challenge to take full advantage of the spectacular terrain and all of the unique attributes the property had
to offer, to preserve as much of the land in its natural state
as possible, and to creatively overcome certain design con-
straints to create the best golf and residential community
in the world. Every hole on the golf course was custom designed and built with extreme care, as was each homesite.
The result was a harmonious blend of natural terrain, an
exciting golf course, and homes that are the best that can be
built. Challenge met.

The Bridges property is essentially a series of islands di-
vided by deep and beautiful canyons that are teeming with
wildlife. When I purchased the property, it was viewed as
literally undevelopable because of the formidable obstacles presented by the canyons. My development concept
was to tie the islands together with a series of bridges,
hence the name.

And that is what we did. The bridge engineering and
construction process was extraordinary, using an elegant
solution of cable suspension bridges to span the canyons
where possible, thereby leaving the canyons in pristine condition to forever preserve a habitat for the abundant
wildlife on the property.

Building the Bridges development required massive
grading and infrastructure construction. To accomplish this
task, we imported mining equipment from Alaska to do
the heavy grading required to turn this vision into reality.

The necessary equipment was so large that special permits were required to transport the machines in the middle of the night from San Diego harbor to Rancho Santa Fe. For example, our Caterpillar trucks weighed in excess of 350,000 pounds when loaded with material. For context, this is the same weight as a fueled-up Boeing 747 airplane. We moved nearly 1,000,000 cubic yards of rock and soil to create the Bridges.

The Bridges development can be viewed online at www.thebridgesrsf.com and I think the reader will agree that there are few communities in the world that are quite like this wonderful place. I am proud to have created the vision for this community from the beginning and enjoyed bringing it to life. This unique community has had a positive impact on Rancho Santa Fe, San Diego County, the lives of our club members, our homeowners, and the incomparable staff at the Bridges.

There were certainly some bumps in the road on the way to turning this vision into reality, including a prolonged and deep recession in California from early 1990 to the end of 1997. In that time period, the real estate market would not support development of my project, and capital was scarce and expensive. But real estate is a never-ending cycle, and by the mid 1990's there were signs of recovery.

In 1995 I had been involved in a number of discussions with various real estate investment funds to participate in a restructure, expansion, and continued development of the Bridges. California was turning the corner and was poised to recover right about that time, and timing is everything in real estate development.

The general landscape at that point in time regarding real estate project financing was a market dominated by aptly named vulture funds. These buzzards were sitting on poles all over California hoping to pick off real estate road-kill from the recession. I had no interest in dealing with these types of high-priced short-term capital sources, and the people who run them. The deals never work out for anyone but them.

In the afternoon of August 16, 1995 while in San Diego, I received a call from Kent Rowett, a top-flight real estate investment banker based in San Francisco. He asked if I could be available for dinner that evening up in the city. I asked, of course, the purpose of the dinner, and he told me there was a representative of an east coast builder in town that evening and that we should meet to discuss a re-capitalization and expansion of the Bridges development.

The dinner meeting was set that evening for a San Francisco restaurant called the Palio D'Asti on Sacramento St. The Palio is a classic and highly regarded northern Italian restaurant with great food and an extensive and well chosen wine list. It was easy to talk me into going up there for dinner, meeting or no meeting.

The builder was Lennar Corporation from Miami, a middle-of-the-pack NYSE-listed entry and mid-level home builder. Lennar had decided to expand their homebuilding operations to California hoping to take advantage of depressed land prices and to get positioned for an anticipated market recovery.

Lennar's representative was a vice president named Jon

Jaffe. We chatted for a while, ordered dinner and a few bot-
tles of wine, and began a discussion about the real estate
in Rancho Santa Fe and the opportunity.

Jaffe definitely did not have the California look: he was
dressed in what turned out to be the typical Lennar uni-
form: inexpensive and poorly tailored suit, white button-
down shirt, nondescript tie, and a name tag. Kind of a
door-to-door salesman's ensemble that also included an ill-
fitting and comically askew hairpiece.

Nonetheless, on the surface, Jaffe can be an engaging
guy, and the conversation was worthwhile because it was
clear Lennar had pockets full of money and wanted in to
the real estate capital-starved California market. And they
wanted to build, unlike the vulture funds. Jaffe professed a
desire to develop and build along the lines I described, so
that was positive. The general terms we discussed were reasonable. Little did I know then what the consequences of
this meeting would hold for the future.

Our dinner discussion revolved around the location and
the economics of the Rancho Santa Fe development, and
why top golf course design professionals working with me
viewed the property as an opportunity to build one of the
great golf courses in the world. And homes to match. Either I must have been persuasive or we all drank too much,
because after dinner we went to the investment banker's
office a few blocks away and negotiated and signed a preliminary agreement. The agreement included an obligation
for Lennar to provide funds the very next day to reserve
the exclusive right to participate in a restructuring and
build-out of the planned development with me.

THE RESTRUCTURING PROCESS got underway in 1995, but took a bit longer than anticipated. By the fall of 1997 the process was nearly complete and we were ready to recommence development of the project in the spring of 1998. We anticipated that it would take up to 10 years to complete and sell out the development based on our conservative pricing and absorption model.

Prior to Lennar's involvement with me, over $65,000,000 of capital had been invested in the Rancho Santa Fe property, including extensive on-site and off-site infrastructure construction. Most of the heavy lifting was done, and the project was primed for a highly profitable completion and sellout. Just waiting for the markets' inevitable turn.

Along the way, Lennar and I retained Gary London of Gary London and Associates to independently analyze and validate the economics of the development and to prepare a development business plan. Mr. London is a highly regarded real estate analyst, investor, speaker, expert witness, and is quoted widely in various publications. His firm is located in San Diego. Adoption of this plan was a requirement in our development company operating agreement.

Our newly-formed development company also engaged the services of Winchester Development, a high-end golf course and residential developer and project manager with an excellent track record in the industry. The Winchester Development partners provided critical expertise to this unique project, and Ken Ayres and Craig Bryant of Winchester brought their considerable energy and ability to the process of developing the golf course and homesites. Their portfolio of successful and notable developments was impressive. This was good, because Lennar's personnel had no local knowledge or any expertise working in true high-end golf and residential communities. At times as we went forward the education process with them was like trying to teach pigs to fly.

The Bridges development was timed perfectly. The moribund California real estate market began reviving and pent-up demand propelled strong sales from the day we released our first homesites and club memberships.

As my company's original land planning and designs leaped from paper to reality, they proved to be outstanding and very well received. The construction process was turning my dream into an extraordinary one-of-a-kind community. And the quality of the development was head and shoulders above any competition. Sales of memberships and homesites got off to a brisk start at prices and at a pace that were far in excess of our internal projections. Finally, a project I had envisioned in 1985 when I bought the land and designed the development was coming to life. Things couldn't be better. Or so it seemed.

Lennar's primary role in the development process was daily management, including responsibility for maintaining separate and dedicated venture bank accounts, implementing and following the jointly-approved London-prepared business plan to develop the property, and providing a detailed monthly report to our jointly-owned company that included revenues, expenditures, plus a general development status update.

My role was that I provided the planning and vision for the development, access to the land, the previously approved masterplan and entitlements, valuable completed infrastructure construction, and a substantial capital investment of over $37,000,000.

It was of utmost importance to me from the very beginning that our development plan respect the unique parcel of land we were fortunate to own. And that most of the site would remain green, natural, and harmonious with our surroundings upon completion of the development. Along these lines, I had previously donated over 200 acres to a conservancy to preserve our beautiful canyons in perpetuity.

The vision from the first day planning commenced for this development was that we design and build in a timeless and top-quality fashion with architectural forms and materials that will withstand the test of time and only improve with age. Stone and rock seemed like the best choice of building materials to me since this durable material has been sitting around relatively unchanged for about 4.9 billion years.

Check the Bridges website. The result speaks for itself. The Bridges Club hosted the internationally televised Battle at the Bridges tournament with Tiger Woods annually for three years, and the show highlighted the incredible golf course and community we built. The tournament was a three hour prime-time event broadcast to the U.S. and dozens of other countries, and included a dramatic nighttime finish under the lights.

Looking at the development today, there is little doubt my company's and my goal of creating timeless and quality architecture, design, and construction that will withstand the test of time has been more than achieved.

It is said that anybody can build a stage but it is the actors that make the play. This is true in the club business as well. We followed this principle as we prepared to open the magnificent club we were building. Winchester's and my focus was on finding and hiring the best staff available to run our club. And we did just that. From the day we opened the club we were the best in the business and our operational style became a model for a number of clubs in the region.

It is important to note that all of the design, most of the key infrastructure construction, and the operational concepts for the Bridges development were completed long before I ever heard of Lennar, and that Lennar had nothing whatsoever to do with the land planning, conceptual underpinnings, permitting of the project, or construction of the massive infrastructure on and off the site.

WHEN LENNAR BECAME daily manager of the development in 1998, they were tasked primarily with adopting and following the agreed business plan prepared by Mr. London, and building in accordance with the design concepts I provided. The London Business Plan that Jon Jaffe on behalf of Lennar and I agreed to projected a gross profit of over $89,000,000 based on the most conservative possible cost and revenue assumptions. In other words, this was the minimum projected earnings capacity. And it turned out that our revenue assumptions went through the

roof as our prices doubled and tripled based on strong demand, superior design, and thoughtful execution.

Our business plan was not complicated. We sold homesites, single family homes, and club memberships. Like any
other business, if we sell our products for less than our
cost, we lose money. If we sell for more than our costs, we
make money. It is that simple.

Based on strong demand, our opening prices for homesites and memberships soared to twice or more above our
initial projections, and some prices, like golf memberships,
eventually rose to five times the initial projections. I had already expensed costly infrastructure construction, and go-
forward costs were under control under the capable and
experienced management of the Winchester people.

Substantial additional revenue derived from our dramatic price increases should have worked its way right to
the bottom line . . . but there was no bottom line according to Lennar's version of the accounting.

Unfortunately, something had happened on the way to
the bank. It turned out the Lennar execs had their own
undisclosed plan and hidden agenda. This was my intro-
duction to the "Lennar Way."

And it turned out that having Lennar in the role of handling money and managing venture bank accounts was like
having Bernie Madoff run your investment portfolio. One
of my obligations in our equally-owned development company was to contribute $37,500,000 in cash to our devel-
opment company. I made this contribution, and Lennar
secretly transferred the entire sum, to the penny, into their
own accounts the same day the funds were wired in. And

I have never seen it since. That is a lot of money, but it was eventually just a small percentage of what Lennar looted from my company, me, and the development.

One of the management duties Lennar undertook was to provide a comprehensive monthly report on project progress, including detailed cost and revenue numbers. The first monthly report prepared by Lennar on behalf of the venture became available in the fall of 1999, about the same time revenue from a number of sources began to flow into the development company.

When my wholly-owned development company, Briarwood Capital LLC, received the first financial report, questions immediately arose regarding Lennar's accounting procedures. Their handling of venture funds, payment of excessive management fees to themselves, unauthorized interest charges levied by Lennar, and the unapproved transfer of venture funds to unrelated Lennar subsidiaries raised serious concerns. Of course, none of this comported with the agreed business plan.

Jon Jaffe provided a number of excuses for these alarming numbers, including "growing pains" at Lennar, accounting "mistakes" by them, and Jaffe agreed to get to the bottom of the problem and take corrective action. These were the first of a long line of ever-more-ridiculous excuses provided by Jaffe to cover the continuous misappropriation of venture funds by Lennar.

The problems were serious enough, and the numbers were big enough, that, just to be safe, it was necessary for me to engage a law firm to work on the problem and to hire a forensic accountant to review the underlying accounting entries that formed the basis for the initial report. The lawyers' and the forensic accountants' reports were not pretty.

Cash was going somewhere, but it was impossible to figure out where from the monthly reports. The forensic accountant made every effort to obtain in-depth accounting numbers, but at the direction of Jaffe and other Lennar executives, Lennar made it difficult or impossible to obtain any meaningful accounting information. Jaffe began a long process of shifting from excuse to excuse to avoid producing the accounting entries necessary to ascertain where the development company's cash was going. The forensic accountant eventually testified that Lennar *never* provided useful information to explain where hundreds of millions of dollars had vanished.

Meanwhile, the Bridges development was a runaway success, sales were far in excess of projection, and the project eventually exceeded revenue expectations by threefold or more. In fact, initial gross revenue projections have been exceeded by over $500,000,000 as of this writing.

Although the accounting issues were important, execution of the development plan was my focus at that time. Accounting errors can be remedied, but flawed execution cannot. And that focus on execution paid off. Promises were made to prospective homebuyers and club members, and promises were going to be kept. And they were.

Despite the clearly stellar financial performance of the development, Jon Jaffe, the Lennar manager, has stated under oath on several occasions that the development was a failure from inception and simply could not and did not ever turn a profit.

It was a replay of the "we all lost" story CEO Stuart Miller told Diane Olick on CNBC about LandSource.

And speaking of Stuart Miller, he testified in regard to the anticipated profitability of the Bridges development. On May 23, 2012 Miller testified:

Q. Did Lennar expect this project (the Bridges) to be profitable?
A. Yes.
Q. Very profitable?
A. Yes.

And it was. For Lennar.

AS PREVIOUSLY MENTIONED, it was agreed that the development of the Bridges project would be governed according to the adopted business plan. And that any substantive deviation from the plan would have to be by mutual agreement.

Jaffe and I participated quite actively in preparation of the London-prepared business Plan, as, of course, did Mr. London. But when a dispute arose over the disposition of project funds, which included diversion of funds to Lennar's accounts in direct contravention of both the agreements and the business plan, Jaffe's solution was to brazenly deny that he participated in preparation of the agreed London Business Plan or that it governed our relationship. This was a lie, as is easily proven by simply reviewing and comparing Mr. Jaffe's and Mr. London's testimony under oath:

On September 9, 2009, Jaffe testified under oath:

"Just to be clear, I don't consider that [April] London plan the business plan" . . .

But Mr. London who prepared the project's business plan at the direction of both Jaffe and me, and who remained involved with the development, had his own observations. Here is his sworn testimony on the same subject:

Q. Did you ever meet alone with Mr. Jaffe before April 22nd, 1998?

A. Yes.

Q. Where did you meet with Mr. Jaffe?

A. I met with him at least once alone in his office in Mission Viejo — I guess it was Mission Viejo.

Q. What was the purpose of your meeting with Mr. Jaffe alone in his office before April 22nd, '98?

A. He had invited me up, and I guess we had dual purposes. One was to continue our discussion about the (Bridges) development and the business plan, and the other was, I think he was reaching out to me and introducing me to Lennar and his staff with the spirit that we'd be working together for some time to come.

Q. Do you recall whether the three of you, you and Mr. Marsch and Mr. Jaffe, met in Mr. Jaffe's office between the time frame December '97 and April 22nd, '98?

A. We had on at least one occasion.

Q. Do you recall any specifics of that meeting?

A. No, not really. Again, just discussions, continuing discussions, about the development plan and the business plan.

Q. Were Mr. Marsch — During this time frame between December '97 and April 22nd, '98, can you remember at all whether Mr. Marsch and Mr. Jaffe were in agreement as to the assumptions they were talking with you about on a going-forward basis, or were they at odds in terms of what assumptions they were instructing you to use in the iterations to come?

A. I would characterize none of the discussions as at odds. Certainly there was give and take of opinion and ideas, but my view of these guys is that they were — they were shoulder to shoulder on this deal. They were partners. They were creating a long-term development plan, and they were working together.

Q. Continue.

A. They were working together, and I was — I was a player in that, in working with them, but I was the hired player. I was also taking instructions from them as to how to proceed with these business plans.

And Mr. London testified as to how successful the Bridges development had become over time:

"The Bridges — the interesting thing about all of this for me, in this testimony, is that we were all wrong about these numbers. The Bridges did fabulously well over the years. Its timing was just about as perfect as it could be, and essentially lots were being sold during the uptick in the real estate market over most of this, over most of this beginning of this century.

And he further testified:

Q. What did you later learn about how accurate you and others were in terms of your projections about The Bridges property?

A. Well, as I said a moment ago, we were all wrong. The Bridges outperformed these models substantially.

And Jaffe certainly understood the basic purpose of our jointly owned Bridges development company, which was to make money.

Here is his sworn testimony on August 31, 2009:

Q. And in fact, one of HCC's (our Bridges development company) purposes was to make money; right?

A. Yes.

Q. Wouldn't that be really HCC's primary purpose as a business, to make money; true?

A. Yes.

So Jaffe acknowledged that the general idea behind my associating with Lennar in this venture was to make money. Duh! And he shared in the preparation of a business plan by a top outside professional that indicated an $89,000,000 gross profit. At worst case. And the ultra-conservative revenue assumptions in that business plan were substantially exceeded as time passed.

But on June 1, 2012 Jaffe testified under oath:

Q. And I imagine Lennar expected this project (the Bridges) to be profitable?

A. Yes.

Q. Has the project been profitable?

A. No, it has not.

On August 13, 2012 Jaffe testified again under oath:

Q. Now, as I understand it, the Bridges development lost money every year since Lennar became involved with HCC (the Bridges development company) and Mr. Marsch; correct?

A. I believe that is correct.

Q. And that is true for every year beginning with 1998; right?

A. Right.

Somebody is not telling the truth about adoption of the business plan and the profitability of the development. That would be Jaffe. He testified that on his watch, under his direct supervision, the Bridges development essentially started losing money within minutes of his appointment as manager. And Jaffe is the same Lennar manager who personally participated in and worked hard on a business plan and earnings projections prepared for the development by a top professional real estate analyst, Mr. London. And later denied he had done so.

We had the wind at our backs from the first day Lennar and I resumed development of the Bridges project. The timing was perfect. We hired an outside professional, Mr. London, to check and recheck the validity of our operating assumptions before proceeding with the project. If I thought there was even a moderate risk of losing money, I certainly would not have risked a capital contribution of

$37,500,000 in cash. It turned out that the unforeseen risk was not the market, it was doing business with Lennar.

Question: What went wrong the moment Jaffe was in place as manager? Stuart Miller and Jon Jaffe both testified that they thought the Bridges development would be quite profitable.

Answer: the same thing that always goes wrong whenever Jaffe and Lennar are put in place as a manager with access to the valuable assets and the checkbook of the next victim.

In reality, the record ultimately showed that Lennar was methodically looting our company from the first dollar of revenue received and reporting continuous losses to cover the theft. At Jaffe's direction, Lennar Corporation itself and unaffiliated Lennar subsidiaries were draining our development company's cash flow as fast as it came in.

There were over fifteen Lennar "pigs" at the trough at one time or another! Maybe these pigs couldn't fly, but they could sure slurp up cash. And in most cases with these unaffiliated subsidiaries, there were no contracts, no work performed, no services provided, and no justification for anything other than, at most, token fees and cost reimbursements.

In addition, Lennar also cooked up and charged outlandish and unauthorized management fees and interest charges against the development in direct contravention of written agreements. And worse, they then purported to "loan" the purloined money back to the development at outlandish interest rates.

KNOWING WHAT WE now know, one must wonder about the working environment at Lennar with people like Miller and Jaffe in charge? And it takes more than just Miller and Jaffe to operate the company in this fashion.

A well-placed whistleblower within Lennar wrote to me in November of 2008 detailing numerous fraudulent and criminal practices, directed specifically by Miller and Jaffe, and carried out by others within the company. More on that in Chapter 10.

There are numerous blogs by ex-Lennar employees discussing the oppressive working environment at Lennar. Many of them are offended by Lennar's unethical business practices. Others detail the atmosphere of fear of retribution if an employee should question Lennar's methods of doing business.

Here are just a few opinions gleaned from employees who reviewed their Lennar work environment on glassdoor.com: *"Worst company I've ever worked for . . . period." "Abrasive upper management." "Management is a dictatorship that treats its employees disrespectfully." "Management are horrible."*

Further blog comments by Lennar's former employees across the country are remarkably consistent. They stress the same themes repeatedly: the work environment at Lennar is *"rife with fraud"*, working there is a *"horrible experience"*, *"emotionally and mentally devastating"*, *"they will rip you off and make YOU pay in the end"*, *"not paying their contractors on time if at all"*, *"they instilled fear in people"* *"the leadership is a bunch of crooks"*, *"an abusive atmosphere"*, *"I can't even begin to express how badly they treat their employees"*, *"the company is ruthless and uncaring"*, *"the homes they sell are substandard and are shoddily constructed with inferior materials and workmanship."*

A simple internet search confirms all of this. You will find recent sites like mylennarlemon.org or ripoffreport.com on which former Lennar employees band together with livid homebuyers to discuss not just the company's penchant for lying, but their borderline illegal employment demands wherein they squeeze employees to the breaking point, resulting in a mind-boggling turnover rate.

Comments are often focused on the relationship between Miller and Jaffe. A number of on-line posts captured the relationship quite well by simply referring to Jaffe as Stuart Miller's *Mini-Me*.

Miller, in turn, referred to Jaffe in analyst conference calls as Lennar's *Plow Horse*. Jaffe acknowledged this in testimony taken on September 9, 2009:

Q. Well, some people — you've been described as the plow horse of the company. Is that one of the descriptions you've been given?

A. I've been called that.

We are definitely not talking about Sea Biscuit here, but, whatever you want to call him, let's look at the track record of this *Plow Horse* and the rest of his stable.

CHAPTER FIVE

The Best and The Brightest

THE AGREEMENT BETWEEN Lennar and my company required a separate and independent project manager. But Lennar executives needed a way to gain unrestricted access to our development company checkbook. So on January 15, 1998, I received a duplicitous letter from Marc Chasman, a typical Lennar executive. Chasman could best be described as Jon Jaffe's "Mini-Mini-Me." And why not? It seems fair: Miller gets one, why shouldn't Jaffe?

The letter from Chasman was designed to promote the concept of hiring Lennar as daily manager of the Bridges development, rather than an outside independent company. In the look-back process it is obvious that this letter was the tool designed to get access to the Bridges development company's cash and set up the Lennar looting process of the development.

But the sales pitch in the letter is all about the efficiencies to be gained by pooling and sharing certain supervisorial personnel with other Lennar-managed ventures. To save

money. And in the context of that sales pitch the Chasman
letter states:

> *"Our belief is that we can be more cost
> effective and bring a higher level of tal-
> ent to bear on our joint ventures by uti-
> lizing our core group of associates to
> substitute for what otherwise would be
> direct employees of the venture."*
>
> *"Subjectively, we believe that our
> system permits more seasoned and ex-
> perienced individuals to collaborate on
> each of our assets."*
>
> *"We believe that the investment will
> perform better in a structure whereby the
> best and brightest of each of our Cali-
> fornia organization's disciplines is over-
> seeing a limited local group dedicated
> solely to the project."*

Mr. Marsch — you are in luck! You can have access to
our "best and brightest." And, with our best and brightest
at the helm, what could possibly go wrong? After all, they
are seasoned and experienced! And, the investment (meaning my $37,500,000) will perform better. Right.

So Jaffe's right-hand man, Chasman, who doesn't ex-
hale without permission from Jaffe, is actually setting the
table for the wholesale looting of the Bridges development
through a myriad of Lennar affiliates who were pigs at the
trough from the day Lennar gained access to the Bridges

development company's solid cashflow.

And the best and brightest, according to Jaffe's sworn testimony, managed to lose money *"every day since Lennar became involved with the Bridges development company."* For ten years straight.

Of course the implication is also that there were employees at Lennar who didn't qualify as best and brightest. Imagine if they had assigned those Lennar employees to the task? Would the result have been any different? How could you tell?

The reality is this: in prolonged rising real estate market conditions like we were fortunate enough to be experiencing, trained monkeys can make money in real estate development. Even trained plow horses could do well. Except Jaffe. At the Bridges. Strikingly, Lennar reported consistent positive earnings at the corporate level during the entire time they reported "losses" at the Bridges development. Coincidence?

Can you imagine a meeting a few years into the Bridges development process that went something like this? Jaffe is moderating the meeting.

OK, first let's have roll call:
Best?—All Here!
Brightest?—We're Here!
Seasoned?—Ready To Go!
Experienced?—Present and Accounted For!
OK, let's get started. Got your name tags on? Good. Now, as you know, we manage the Bridges development in Rancho Santa Fe and it is clear that we have lost money every day since we undertook

management of the development. Mr. Miller is very concerned about this, since he thought this would be a very profitable opportunity, as I did, and when he is concerned, I am concerned. We have responsibilities to our partner, so this must be resolved right now. Let me go around the table and try to figure this out:

Q. Best — is it the market?

A. No. The market is great. The wind is at our backs. It just keeps getting better.

Q. Brightest — Is it pricing?

A. No. We have actually doubled our business plan prices and there is room on the upside for more increases.

Q. Seasoned — Is it costs?

A. Nope, Mr. Marsch built and expensed most of the heavy front-end costs, and part of our responsibilities are to manage costs on a go-forward basis. Our margins are huge. But I could do some spreadsheets, prepare some memos, and have some meetings, if that would help.

Q. Experienced — What's going on?

A. We don't know. Never seen anything like it.

Well, I can't see this meeting happening either. Apparently Miller and Jaffe, although they testified that their expectations were that the Bridges development would be unusually profitable, were, alas, more than content to "lose money" for ten years in a row. What do you think?

And Miller and Jaffe tried everything they could think of to enhance the Bridges bottom line: Miller bought a jet, Jaffe got a lavish home in Laguna Beach, a helicopter, opened some offshore accounts, but nothing seemed to work.

Now, imagine what was going on in the 300 or so other

Lennar off-balance sheet joint ventures. Unexpected losses?
Check. Bogus accounting? Most likely. Lennar pigs at the
trough? No doubt. As the whistleblower letter writer recounted:

*"As a manager, I have witnessed endless improprieties made by
Stuart Miller, Jon Jaffe, and management."*

*"I am finding countless abuse(s) and improper accounting treat-
ment"*

JON JAFFE IS the living proof of the old maxim that "the
key to success is sincerity. Once you can fake that, you've
got it made." Early in the relationship he handed me a mirror with the following inscription engraved into the front:

*"When you get what you want in your struggle for self
And the world makes you king for a day,
just go to the mirror and look at yourself
and see what that man has to say!*

*For it isn't your father or mother or wife
Whose judgement upon you must pass,
The fellow whose verdict counts most in your life
is the one staring back in the glass.*

*Some people may think you are a straight shootin'
chum
And call you a wonderful guy,
But the man in the glass says you're only a bum*

if you can't look him straight in the eye.

He's the fellow to please never mind all the rest
For he's with you clear to the end
And you've passed the most dangerous difficult test
if the man in the glass is your friend.

You may fool the whole world down the pathway of
life
And get pats on the back as you pass,
But your final reward will be heartaches and tears
if you've cheated the man in the glass."

LENNAR — Family of Builders

Copies of this mirror in various sizes, some small and some very large, adorn Lennar offices coast to coast. The message was clear: we are honest people, dripping with "integrity", and you can trust us to honor our agreements. Well, when someone or some organization goes out of their way to tell you how honest they are, chances are they are not. Unfortunately, the back side of the mirror is blank, so that may have been the side Jaffe was reading.

Somewhere along the line Jaffe had been promoted to Chief Operating Officer of Lennar, but the evasion continued. Meanwhile, our demands continued for an accurate accounting for what had become hundreds of millions of dollars of revenue, and the excuses offered by Jaffe became more and more ridiculous. The requests for an accurate in-depth accounting from Lennar began in 1999, the requests were continuously stonewalled, sidestepped, or ignored. And here are Jaffe's verbatim excuses offered as late as fall 2006:

> *November 3, 2006— "Hey Nick it's Jon Jaffe . . . I want to try and catch up with you. Brian Bilzen (counsel to Lennar) called me today, told me about a conversation with (lawyer) Brian Foster and give me a call back but in case we have a hard time hooking up I want to apologize and I really feel badly that we've not been responsive to you. No excuse, but as you know the housing market is in just absolute free fall and definitely . . . factor with that but I will promise you that I will put . . . this weekend and we'll get it wrapped up hopefully the middle of next week at the earliest and last of the week at the latest but by next week I will get you the information you are looking for. If you are already on a course and feel you need to do what you need to do I understand and respect it, hopefully it doesn't come to that but I understand your frustration and again apologize for it. So if you like give me a call. In any event either way we will get the information to you next week. Thanks. Bye."*
>
> *November 13, 2006— "Nick, I tried to reach you a few times to let you know that I had heard from Brian Bilzen that you were proceeding with litigation. I want to again apologize for the timing in getting information to you. As I mentioned in my voice mail I had our people work on getting the reconciliation of numbers for the Bridges. The only rea-*

*son it did not go out to you as I promised
is that Bob Strudler, our chairman,
passed away on Tuesday. This unfortunate event took me out of the office to
attend the funeral and spend time with
his family. I am back today and committed to reviewing the work that was
done to insure that it is complete and will
forward it on to you. I'm sorry we were
not able to get this to you last week, but
hope that you will appreciate the distraction of Bob's passing. Jon."*

I get it. The chairman was working hard on the numbers and suddenly slumped over. A very creative excuse. Couldn't Stuart Miller have taken over? Not surprisingly, no numbers were ever forthcoming. I felt like I was waiting for Godot.

In business one is, at some point, faced with being at the crossroads of a clear trade-off of success at the price of betrayal of trust. It is clear what road Jaffe has taken.

Jaffe's M.O. is to approach every potential business relationship for the company in the "Lennar Way." Say or do whatever it takes to engage in a relationship, get control of valuable assets and the checkbook, loot the venture down to its last dollar, and if the victim complains, litigate until they give up, shut up, go broke, or go away.

Jaffe testified under oath on March 24, 2010 that he did not read the Bridges development company primary operating agreement before signing it. Or ever. Their CFO, Mike White, said the same — never read the agreement.

What would be the point of reading agreements if he and the company had no intention of honoring the agreements in the first place? And they surely did not. In fact, how could they honor the terms of an agreement if they never read it in the first place?

Lawsuits are routinely filed across the country against Lennar over their dishonest business practices. The complaints generally demand honest accountings, adherence to and compliance with agreements, and often return of misappropriated funds.

The Lennar response in our case was to hire the most vicious and unprincipled lawyers on earth and commence scorched-earth litigation, using, among other techniques, resource exhaustion and character assassination.

This has been my exact experience with Lennar. And it has cost me well over $100,000,000 in hijacked capital, lost profits, and legal fees. Not to mention incalculable reputational damage and emotional distress, the loss of future revenue, as well as the loss of benefits accrued by decades of hard work.

Filing litigation was ultimately the only remaining option available to me to obtain an accounting for over $500,000,000 in revenue. And what followed is an extraordinary tale about a perfect storm of corporate greed and deception, abuse and corruption of the rule of law and the legal process, and the lengths Lennar Corp, its executives and its lawyers were willing and continue to be willing to go to cover up a series of fraudulent and criminal acts by them targeting their partners, lenders and others who have done business with this company.

Useful insights into Jon Jaffe's character, or more accurately, lack of character, are readily available from observation of his actions, his track record, and his carefully coached and mendacious testimony under oath in various proceedings. Read on.

CHAPTER SIX

A Masters in Mendacity

"Mendacity: lack of honesty, lying, perjury, deceit, misrepresentation, duplicity, insincerity, fabrication, and falsehoods"

AFTER EFFORTS TO resolve matters with Lennar went nowhere, and their excuses ran out, I filed two lawsuits in connection with our equally-owned Bridges development company. The purpose of filing the lawsuits was to force a turnover of withheld accounting numbers and to make Lennar account for a lucrative development opportunity misappropriated from our jointly-owned development company.

As part of the litigation process, depositions of Jaffe and other Lennar executives were taken in early 2007 in San Diego. Surprisingly, on January 23, 2007 Jaffe testified:

Q. Okay. How did you get here today, sir?
A. Helicopter.

This was a puzzling answer for a number of reasons. Jaffe lives in Laguna Beach, just 70 miles from downtown San Diego. About an hour drive. And there are paved roads now all the way to San Diego from Orange County. And back. To take a helicopter, he had to first drive from home to the airport in Orange County, then fly to San Diego's airport, then drive to the deposition location in downtown San Diego.

Total time savings: maybe 10 minutes. Cost to shareholders: thousands of dollars. And that was in 2007, a year when Lennar posted its largest loss in the company's history under the astute management of Miller and Jaffe.

Of course, time is money in Jaffe's world. There was money to be lost, partners to cheat, lenders to defraud, and there was no time to waste. We didn't know then that Lennar, with Jaffe as COO, had just finished implementing the FDIC fraud in Ft. Myers, Florida and was gearing up for the LandSource swindle that took place just a few months after the January depositions. More on that in Chapter 8. It was clear from Jaffe's demeanor that he had reached a delusional level of arrogance and self-importance.

Jaffe's background includes a degree in architecture and he also attended but didn't finish a program at Georgia Tech. So, not much in the way of qualifications or certifications to be COO of Lennar, but what he lacked in pedigree he more than made up for in greed and ambition.

Jaffe testified under oath in January 2007 over a three day period on a number of topics. Other Lennar executives testified as well. These depositions did not go well for them or Lennar. He and other executives made a series of damaging admissions that would be difficult to overcome if the litigation process continued. Consequently, a short time later, Lennar's lead lawyer was replaced by Daniel Petrocelli of the O'Melveny & Myers law firm in Los Angeles.

Mr. Petrocelli's initial claim to fame was representing the Goldman family in Los Angeles against O. J. Simpson. And Petrocelli had just wrapped up a failed criminal defense in Houston of his client, Jeffrey Skilling, CEO of Enron. He and his Skilling team were all now available to defend Lennar and its executives including Stuart Miller and Jon Jaffe. Interesting choice. We would find out later why Mr. Petrocelli, among all of the available attorneys in the country, was hired to defend Lennar.

Petrocelli took a new approach to the cases, and apparently it was an approach he had used many time before. The new approach was to create an "alternate universe" where Lennar was a victim, and the other side (in this case me) was reprehensible in every way.

We, of course, did not know this at the time, but the new approach, of necessity, included extensive coaching of the Lennar witnesses to lie under oath and to tailor their testimony to whatever was required to sell the alternate universe theory to a judge or the media.

Taking this approach required a buy-in by the Lennar executives to this process and their complete cooperation. That necessitated that his clients were willing to lie, play dumb, act the part, and above all, be prepared to squander unlimited shareholder money until hell won't have it. Petrocelli had agreed to defend Lennar to its last dollar, but the executives had to do their part. Telling the truth, even under oath, wasn't even a consideration in this process.

Contrast Jaffe's testimony before Petrocelli and his team entered the picture, and then afterwards. Here is Jaffe's testimony taken under oath and verbatim from a deposition taken on January 23, 2007:

Q. You (Jaffe) understand that you're sitting here today under oath, and you're under a legal obligation to answer my questions fully, completely and honestly?

A. Yes.

Q. You understand it's the same oath you take in a courtroom?

A. Yes.

Q. Carries with it the same penalty of perjury if you're untruthful?

A. Yes.

Q. In the ten years or so that you've worked with Mr. Marsch, did he ever tell you anything that you later learned to be untrue?

A. I am not aware of any situations where Mr. Marsch ever lied to me, no.

And on January 24, 2007, Jaffe testified under oath:

Q. . . . Did you think he (Mr. Marsch) did anything unfair or wasn't nice or inappropriate or illegal or unethical or immoral or anything at all?

A. No. I can't think of anything he did that I would consider wrong.

Q. I mean, he certainly treated Lennar with integrity on this transaction, didn't he?

A. To the best of my knowledge, he did.

Then in a deposition taken on June 1, 2012, here was Jaffe's new story after extensive coaching by Petrocelli:

"Most of the things he said to me are not true."

And variations of this newly-minted theme have been repeated *ad nauseum* in countless legal papers, court hearings, and press releases. All part of the character assassination undertaken by Petrocelli with the enthusiastic approval and cooperation of Lennar.

By the time Jaffe testified under oath in 2007, he and I had been working together for over ten years. "Shoulder to shoulder," in the words of Gary London. We socialized on occasion, even traveling together now and then. He ate our food, accepted our hospitality, his family even used our home periodically. I even tried to teach Jaffe to surf (entertaining), ski (even more entertaining), and even how to navigate a wine list and order a bottle of wine. And I gave him the benefit of the doubt over his endless and threadbare excuses about accounting issues. I didn't know he had perfected the art of shaking your hand with one hand and picking your pocket with the other.

The litigation process that began in late 2006 continued and eventually the Bridges matter went to trial. During the trial, the Lennar executives each had handlers to provide appropriate coaching and rehearsed testimony. It was imperative to keep the story straight.

Jaffe's coached demeanor in the Bridges trial was that

of the rube who didn't know much, couldn't remember much, was misled, taken for a ride, and taken in by the local sharpie (me) and his confederates. Never mind that they kept the books and bank accounts, and were managing the development process.

Jaffe was portrayed by his lawyers to be like the would-be starlet getting off the bus in Hollywood fresh from Kansas and getting hustled immediately on arrival:

Jeepers Mister, you mean I can be in your movie? Sure kid, just hop in and let's go for a ride.

Jeepers Mister Marsch, you mean I can be in your development? Sure kid, just sign here.

Even the would-be starlet might have figured out what was actually going on if she stopped, got dressed, and had *10 years* to think about it.

Remember, this is the same Jaffe who took CALPERS and Barclays Bank for a billion dollar ride like two kids in the backseat. And he is the highly-paid Lennar executive who started the California operation and hand-selected the best and brightest for Lennar.

So Jaffe was on his way to getting his Masters in Mendacity. And in the Petrocelli-created alternate universe, Jaffe's new mantra was that Marsch was now a liar, a crook, and a hustler, and Lennar was a victim. Even though Lennar exclusively kept the books, records, managed venture bank accounts — and made money disappear faster than a Las Vegas magician.

Much of the coached testimony given by Jaffe and other Lennar executives that flowed from this arrangement bor-

dered on the absurd. Jaffe and other Lennar execs were instructed to disregard the truth and simply parrot whatever alternate universe explanations that were concocted by
Petrocelli and his team. But even after hours of coaching,
they couldn't keep the story straight on the witness stand.

So the next thing that happened in that courtroom was
simply astounding. The Lennar lawyers devised an elaborate
signaling scheme to coach the Lennar execs on the witness
stand and signal the right answer. The signals between
lawyer/handler and witness were generally horizontal or ver-
tical: eyebrows up or a perceptible head nod meant yes, side-
ways headshake or hand motion meant no. Think about how
binary the answers "yes" or "no" are. One is the opposite
of the other, but the Lennar executives had to be told which
was correct? Amazing.

Never mind the truth, just follow the script. So, essentially, the Lennar lawyers were testifying, the testimony was
manufactured, and that procedure completely undermined
the integrity of the process and the validity of any trial result.

Again, you might think this story is farfetched, because,
after all, what judge would allow such a perversion of the
legal system, and simply let Lennar's lawyers de facto testify
instead of their clients? The answer is that the trial judge did
exactly that. Here is a verbatim passage from a court transcript taken on September 9, 2009 with Jon Jaffe on the witness stand under oath in cross examination:

*Q. Mr. Jaffe, I notice that every time I ask you a question, you
look to counsel before you answer my question. Is there a reason you
do that?*

This question was followed by the usual volley of objections, and the examining lawyer finally addressed the court directly:

"It's been rather distracting, and I also notice that in order to avoid that, I have to stand right over counsel . . . I'm not sure — because your Honor is a prolific note taker, I'm not sure if your Honor has been able to observe this behavior of the witness, but it has been continual since the first question; and it has created not only a distraction but a question in my mind as to the basis for what appears to be, when I ask a question, the witness' eyes immediately dart over to counsel table and wait for what may be communication or — I don't know what. And the only time it does not occur is when either I ask my question facing counsel or ask my questions behind counsel, and that is a distraction to me. And I don't know that your Honor has been able to observe that because I know your Honor is involved in other matters. I only point it out because it has been constant, and your Honor's roles among others is to assess witness credibility, and I don't know that it has been noticed, but it is an annoyance and

it is perpetual. I just wanted to know
if there was a reason that for every
question — I thought it important to
ask."

This is, of course, very dangerous territory for a plain-tiff's lawyer in the midst of a lengthy and contentious trial. To even suggest that a judge would allow the basic process of seeking truth from a witness or a number of witnesses to be undermined by overt and on-going witness coaching on a continuous basis is a risky proposition, even though it was happening with every single Lennar witness.

So, the examining lawyer's statement to the court is carefully nuanced to avoid offense to the court, while seek-ing relief from a painfully obvious deception taking place in the judge's courtroom that was tantamount to witness tampering. To our absolute shock and surprise, here is the court's response:

"The Court has noticed Mr. Jaffe looking over in Mr. Petrocelli's
direction long before this morning. I don't think it's to the point of
every question, as [the examining lawyer] said. That may be a bit
of hyperbole, but it's been often, and I've noticed it."

Not only did the judge acknowledge the fact that he was personally observing this coaching and signaling process, he acknowledged that it had been going on for days. And he did absolutely nothing about it, allowed the practice to continue, and effectively let the trial record be made with thoroughly false and tainted testimony.

The documents governing our development company relationship with Lennar were prepared by the DLA Piper law firm. No documents are perfect and these definitely weren't. When the parties on both sides of the transaction are acting in good faith, that may not matter. But the Lennar lawyers sought to redefine every word, paragraph and section in the agreements to suit the new Petrocelli alternate universe.

And the judge went on to make a decision based on disregarding each and every term that had been carefully negotiated by the parties, and instead accepted the oral testimony of the Lennar executives in place of the DLA-prepared agreements. And, the Lennar execs weren't even testifying, their lawyers were through an elaborate signaling system.

Jaffe's miserable and unethical conduct was certainly not limited to his deplorable performance in legal proceedings. Let's look at the track record he has compiled as manager in a number of large-scale real estate development projects:

He claims the Bridges development lost money for ten years on his watch. He helped mastermind the disastrous failure of LandSource. He conspired to hijack the Lakes development from our operating company, promptly ran it into the ground, and sold it for a loss.

It is clear that when Jaffe is put in charge of a venture on behalf of Lennar, a train wreck is inevitably just around the next corner. And there are many, many documented examples of similar conduct documented across the country. The record is consistent, and it is appalling.

Based on this plow horse's track record, what company would hire Jaffe to do anything except maybe wash cars in the parking lot? Answer: Lennar. And he is richly compensated. Huge salary. Bonuses in the millions. Stock options. Jets. Helicopters. Cars. Who knows what else? Why: he follows the script, has no scruples, and most importantly follows the Lennar Way every time.

As one views Jon Jaffe through the lens of his own actions and his own testimony, the picture that emerges is not a pretty one. Greed is a disease, and it is contagious. An obsession with wealth is a dead end, and the operative word is dead. There is no point in stealing, lying, and committing fraud all in an effort to become the richest guy in the cemetery.

Jaffe, under the tutelage of Miller, has become emblematic of what is wrong in corporate America. He and Miller, as too many corporate executives do, have traded self-worth for net worth. That is never a good trade. A trade-off of integrity for success. How hollow.

This Faustian bargain was accomplished most often at the expense of others who trusted him. Like me. Remember, he was the guy with the mirror. The true reflection of Lennar's Chief Operating Officer is certainly not a pretty one and as you read on, it just gets worse.

CHAPTER SEVEN

Flim Flam Accounting

IT IS WELL documented that Lennar engaged in a systematic withholding of accounting information from my wholly-owned development company and me. If one reads the various excuses offered by Jaffe, one might think that it was simply an oversight, that he was telling the truth, and a real accounting might be forthcoming. Definitely not the case.

Jaffe was certainly admitting in those communiques that the company had not been responsive to numerous requests for accounting numbers. Excuses like: "*I really feel badly that we've not been responsive to you*", "*The market is in free fall*", "*I will get you the information you are looking for*" and then "*our chairman passed away*" were just a variation of the nonsense Jaffe came up with whenever cornered on the accounting issue.

In actuality Jaffe had no intention of producing reliable numbers because they would reveal massive looting of the venture and unauthorized transfers to other Lennar-controlled affiliates in need of cash.

Our forensic accountant had no luck either in eliciting reliable numbers from Lennar. But not from lack of trying.

And Jaffe and Marc Chasman (Remember him? The "best and the brightest"?) maintained tight control over what Bridges numbers could be shared with us (if any).

In fact, the discovery process turned up a very informative internal Lennar memo authored by Marc Chasman on November 7, 2006 that revealed the true nature of Lennar's information withholding process.

In November 2006, Chasman became aware that a Lennar executive had inadvertently sent me an internal Lennar analysis of certain Bridges development — related numbers. This caused an internal uproar. In an email dated 11-07-2006, Chasman chastised his fellow "best and brightest," stating:

"BIG BIG Mistake." "I am surprised Pete would send this to Nick before I scrub it one more time."

And the implication of this email is that any numbers provided to me had to be "*scrubbed*," and that even though these numbers had already been "*scrubbed*" a number of times, they had not been sufficiently sanitized before dissemination.

Our forensic accountant testified on July 6, 2009:

Q. Did he (an internal Lennar accountant) ever explain to you why it was that Mr. Chasman or Mr. Jaffe would have to review the spreadsheets before you would be allowed to see them?

A. He just said they had to be reviewed before they could be re-leased. No other reason.

And our forensic accountant actually attended a meeting with Lennar accounting people including a senior controller in yet another effort to get numbers. The first statement from this Lennar controller was that *"We can make the numbers whatever we want."* And by *"the numbers"* he meant the reported numbers released to the SEC and Wall Street on a quarterly and annual basis by Lennar. This is known as cooking the books, and here a senior controller was admitting this in advance of a meeting to discuss . . . the books. Hello.

And speaking of flim-flam accounting and cooking the books, here is what came next. When litigation over the Bridges accounting issues commenced, Lennar, on the one hand refused to provide useful internal numbers to us. But, on the other hand, they hired a Los Angeles financial expert firm to re-construct the books and records. At a cost of over two million dollars!

You know — the books and records they had paid themselves handsomely to keep as managers of the development company since 1998. And re-construct to them meant elevating Lennar's "where's-the-pea movie accounting" techniques to a whole new level.

It was a fact that Lennar was required under our agreements to keep separate books, records, and bank accounts. They did none of the above, and instead commingled our projects' funds with their own. We are talking about many hundreds of millions of dollars. And then they tried to pass off this practice as cash management. Here is the exact requirement in the primary operating agreement:

"Deposit all receipts from operations or sales of the Company Property to a separate account established and maintained by the Project Manager, and shall not commingle those receipts with any other funds or accounts of Project Manager."

The re-construction of the books made Hollywood movie accounting, long viewed as the most suspect of all industry accounting procedures, look honest by comparison. But even the "re-construction" of the books could not hide the fact that Lennar was directing its subsidiaries and affiliates to loot our company of every available dollar. I felt like Humphrey Bogart in *The African Queen*: I jumped in the Lennar swamp and came out covered with leeches.

Through the litigation discovery process we began to unearth one interesting document after another and eventually pieced together a massive fraud on our development company and other entities managed by Lennar. Money was moving freely from one entity to another without regard to actual ownership of funds and it was becoming clear why the records were withheld from us.

And also what became increasingly clear was that Lennar was looting our venture and several others to assist in pulling off what was maybe the largest real estate-related fraud in California history. Which takes us to the next chapter on LandSource LLC.

CHAPTER EIGHT

LandSource

Swindle: 1. *Use deception to deprive someone of money or possessions.*
2. *A fraudulent scheme or action.*

THIS IS THE real story behind Lennar's looting, destruction, and pennies-on-the-dollar buyout of Land-Source LLC, a large California landholding enterprise organized and managed by . . . Lennar. It was a carefully executed plan to dupe CALPERS — the California Public Employees Retirement System, plus a Barclay's Bank-led bank loan syndicate, the Bankruptcy court in Delaware, over five thousand unsecured LandSource creditors, and numerous managed ventures of Lennar out of well over $1,000,000,000.

And, guess who is in charge on this one? If you guessed Jaffe, you are right. In a deposition taken on January 23, 2007, Jaffe testified:

Q. Have you ever had a position with an entity called Land Source, sir?

A. Yes.

Q. Do you know what your title was?

A. I know that I'm on the executive committee.

Q. Of Land Source?

A. Of Land Source.

Q. Okay. Do you know how it was you came to be on the executive committee of Land Source?

A. I was the logical person because of my being a key decision maker with respect to the activities of LandSource.

LandSource LLC was a landholding company created to hold real property assets for development and sale that was organized, managed, and run right into the ground in record time by Jaffe and Lennar.

Lennar used assets that were contributed to the reorganized LandSource LLC by CALPERS, the giant California employee retirement fund, and a syndicated loan from Barclays Bank, to loot the company to the tune of $1.4 billion dollars. They accomplished this fraud by using inflated appraisals and bogus cash flow projections. In other words, they concealed the true financial condition of the borrower, LandSource, to obtain the funds.

Under Lennar management LandSource was inevitably forced to file bankruptcy after Lennar and its sister company, LNR, loaded the balance sheet of the company with $1.4 billion in debt. Debt they knew at the time LandSource could neither service nor pay back. This loan was funded on March 1, 2007 and Lennar and its sister company paid out the entire amount to themselves as a special dividend the same day the loan was funded. All of this into the teeth of a growing economic storm that showed no signs of abating any time soon.

This special dividend was a one-way ticket to bankruptcy for LandSource. The Lennar executives knew this, and the inevitable bankruptcy filing was all part of their plan.

LandSource had over 5,000 unsecured creditors when Lennar put the company in bankruptcy. The unsecured creditors soon realized that they had been defrauded by Lennar and retained counsel. According to the well-researched and documented lawsuit filed by the committee formed on behalf of these unsecured creditors:

> *"Upon information and belief, the December 2006 appraisals of Land Source's real property conducted by CB Richard Ellis, Inc. ("December 2006 Appraisals") which were used to secure the Barclays Financing overstated the value of LandSource's assets, and contained significant errors and omissions."*
>
> *"Upon information and belief, as sophisticated investors in distressed real estate, LandSource's sole owners LNR and Lennar knew or reasonably should have known that the December 2006 Appraisals overstated the value of*

LandSource's property, and as a result, LandSource's assets were grossly inflated in connection with the February 2007 recapitalization and payment of the $1.4 billion distributions."

"Contrary to the realities of the steep decline in the housing market, LandSource painted a fraudulent picture of its corporate health in order to induce an equity payout to Lennar and LNR under the guise of a recapitalization of the company."

"LandSource was Insolvent and Should Not Have Incurred Additional Debt to Fund the Fraudulent Transfers."

"Immediately prior to entering into the Contribution Agreement, LNR and Lennar, as the sole owners of LandSource, knew that LandSource was insolvent, was about to engage in a transaction for which the remaining assets of LandSource were unreasonably small, and/or believed or reasonably should have believed that LandSource would incur debts beyond its ability to pay as they became due and/or suspected that it would not be able to service its existing debt."

"While it was already insolvent at

*the time of the February 2007 trans-
action, following the transaction, Land-
Source's financial condition quickly fell
into further decline."*

*"The willingness of the Barclay's
investors and MWHP (CALPERS)
to participate in this transaction was
based, in part, on the near-term cash
flow expected from Lennar and LNR's
business plans to purchase the majority of LandSource's property over the
next three years."*

*"Specifically, LandSource's pro-
jected revenue and near-term cash flow
at the time of the 2007 transaction was
heavily dependent on Lennar and
LNR to follow through with their business plans, which never occurred.
Lennar's business plan to provide near-
term cash flow to LandSource, in the
form of purchase contracts, option
agreements, and rights of first offer,
were relied upon to constitute over 70%
of LandSource's revenue for the next
three years. Meanwhile, LNR planned
to acquire 100% of LandSource's
planned commercial land sales for the
next three years."*

*"It would be difficult for anyone to
believe, let alone sophisticated real estate*

*investors like Lennar and LNR, that
LandSource would be able to service the
amount of additional debt it took on
and at the same time make equity dis-
tributions to Lennar and LNR well exceeding the Amount of that additional
debt.*"

All evidence points to the fact that to obtain the loan on behalf of LandSource, Jaffe, as manager, arranged, provided, and signed off on inflated appraisals and knowingly fraudulent cash flow projections to support the loan. He was, by his own admission, a key decision maker.

It is inconceivable that the Lennar executives, you know — the best and brightest— did not know at the time the transaction closed that there was no intention on the part of Lennar or LNR to purchase land or other assets from LandSource, thereby committing fraud in the inducement.

These fraudulent representations aren't too shocking since Lennar had just warmed up for the LandSource swindle by defrauding the FDIC using . . . inflated appraisals and straw buyers in Ft. Myers Florida just a few months earlier.

Again, Miller testified under oath on September 16, 2008:

We are not a reactive company. We are anticipatory in our approach to almost anything . . . we try to do things strategically and by plan.

And there is nothing truer than that statement. Jaffe's communication to me of November 3, 2006: *"the housing market is in just absolute freefall"* was written almost four months before the LandSource loan swindle was finalized and his communication to me was written just two months before the FDIC inflated-appraisal straw-buyer caper.

Given the prevailing economic conditions at that time, what sane and fiduciarily responsible manager of a land holding company would leverage up the balance sheet to the tune of 1.4 billion dollars and implement the immediate removal of all of the cash from the balance sheet, thereby leaving the company overleveraged and completely illiquid at the worst possible time?

Mr. Jaffe and Mr. Miller knew by November 2006 that the housing market was collapsing. And if the housing market was collapsing (and it was) they knew that land markets would follow immediately thereafter (and they did). But they went ahead and were instrumental in leveraging LandSource by providing false and misleading revenue projections and inflated appraisals, extracting desperately needed cash despite the absolute certainty the company would fail and retirees, investors, and creditors would lose their money. How cynical.

There was no way to service or pay this debt and Lennar executives knew it the day they piled the debt on LandSource's balance sheet and stripped all but token cash from the company. Who did they think was going to pay interest on this huge loan or repay the principal? Certainly not the borrower, LandSource.

Neither Jaffe nor Miller could pass the simple Watergate cover-up test question: What did you know, and when did you know it?

But siphoning off the entire proceeds of the loan was okay with Lennar, because the next steps in the well-thought-out-fraud were to put LandSource into bankruptcy in Delaware, far from California, stiff the lenders and the unsecured creditors, lose CALPERS entire investment of nearly $1,000,000,000, and buy back the assets at pennies on the dollar. And they did just that. A tour de force of every flavor of fraud. Fraud in the inducement, fraudulent transfer, financial institution fraud, and bankruptcy fraud.

A BASIC CONCEPT in lending is material change. Most prospective lending arrangements utilize a material change clause that requires the prospective borrower to notify the lender if and when a prospective borrower becomes aware of a material change in the information supplied to the lender in connection with a pending loan transaction. And the concept of material change is implied in any lender/borrower negotiation.

This is especially true if the material change in conditions would adversely affect the underwriting assumptions provided to the lender to induce the lender to lend. And real estate-secured loan underwriting at its core is relatively simple. Lenders have three main criteria that must be satisfied: What is the nature and value of the collateral? How will the borrower pay interest on a timely basis? How and when will the loan be paid back? Clearly there are always other factors in play, but if the proposed borrower can't get past these three hurdles, there is nothing else to talk about.

So it is obvious that the lender, a Barclays Bank syndicate, was fraudulently induced to lend. And equally obvious that CALPERS's assets were being used to implement this scheme. Then, because the special dividend rendered Land-Source immediately insolvent, the special dividend was a fraudulent transfer of assets out of LandSource.

The term special dividend used in this transaction by Lennar would be not unlike a bank robber tunneling into the bank at night and taking a "special dividend!"

The fact that the special dividend rendered LandSource insolvent the day it was paid created a problem for Lennar: they knew LandSource was insolvent and headed for bankruptcy, and it was only a question of *when?* But *when* is a very, very important question, as we will see.

So far, we have fraud in the inducement, a fraudulent transfer, but like they say on late-night TV: "but wait, there's more!" Onward to the next fraudulent acts orchestrated by Jaffe and Lennar. Had Lennar been forced to put LandSource into bankruptcy anytime less than one year after the loan and special dividend took place, preference rules integral to the bankruptcy process would have required them to put all of the money back into LandSource. Plus interest. That's the law. Good for LandSource, probably fatal to Lennar. LandSource, in fact, filed bankruptcy a mere 14 months after the loan was obtained and the special dividend was paid.

Miller—*"We try to do things strategically and by plan."*

The implementation of the next phase of Lennar's

LandSource scheme then required wholesale theft of money from entities also managed by Lennar. These funds were diverted from Lennar-managed entities to prop up LandSource and mask it's true financial condition long enough to survive the all-important one year preference period.

And it was irrelevant to Lennar whether Lennar was the actual owner of the entities as long as they were the manager and had access to the entity's bank account. Our jointly owned Bridges development company was one of the entities looted by Lennar to prop up LandSource. This company had no loans and no financial arrangements with LandSource. Its only nexus was Jaffe and Lennar.

We have a number of documents obtained through the litigation discovery process that illustrate this point. And these documents were only obtained after a prolonged, expensive, and hotly contested court process. Clearly Lennar had plenty to hide.

Included in these documents are internal Lennar communications and testimony from Lennar's west coast CFO Mike White. Also, a memo dated April 3, 2007 by a Lennar controller starts at the top with the word "OUCH!!!" in big letters, and for good reason. In this memo, the controller details the funds being fraudulently transferred from our company and others to try and service the massive debt piled on LandSource in the wake of the "special dividend." More internal documents obtained from Lennar show millions of dollars being siphoned off from our company to pay interest for a loan that wasn't ours. And never was.

Lennar's west coast CFO, Mike White, was questioned on this matter under oath and here is what he had to say:

Q. (to Mr. White) So to the extent HCC (our jointly-owned Bridges development company) paid money to LandSource for (capped) interest, that was inappropriate, wasn't it?

A. That would be inappropriate, yes.

Q. Any funds that HCC paid to LandSource would be wrong and inappropriate?

A. Yes.

It is abundantly clear from the records that millions and millions of dollars had been siphoned out of our company and improperly transferred to LandSource to support the fraud.

The audacity of this scheme is mind-boggling. Land-Source, under management by Lennar's *best and brightest*, was perhaps the largest single real estate failure in California history. Its failure was no accident or just the result of an unexpected downturn. The failure was the result of a cynical and well planned scheme to enrich Lennar and to defraud and victimize the many California employees who entrusted their retirement savings to CALPERS.

And to defraud and victimize the many debt investors whose funds were pooled by Barclay's Bank and loaned to LandSource. Lennar also defrauded and victimized the suppliers and contractors of LandSource who became unsecured creditors.

They defrauded and victimized the managed joint ventures, like mine, that Lennar looted to prop up LandSource and prevent catastrophic exposure to the one year preference rule in bankruptcy.

It is also worth noting that at the time the LandSource

special dividend was paid, Stuart Miller was President and Chief Executive of Lennar, and also had interests in Lennar's sister company, LNR. And he was former Chairman of LNR. LNR did quite well on this transaction, and thus Miller.

PUBLIC FILINGS INDICATE Lennar Corp was desperate for cash by 2007. The company was overleveraged, was viewed as a "black box" by much of Wall Street, and had hidden exposure to billions in debt through their opaque off-balance sheet ventures. A review of Lennar's 2007 quarterly 10 Q reports filed with the SEC indicates that the nearly $700,000,000 obtained from the special dividend vanished immediately.

This pattern is remarkably similar to Enron's real but undisclosed financial situation, and their huge unreported off-balance sheet exposure. A review of Lennar Corp's public reports indicate a sharp and continuous drop in cash balances in 2007, despite receipt of nearly $700 million. The company was bleeding to death at an alarming rate.

One thing for sure, it is a fact that Lennar could not have followed through with the land acquisition schedule they had submitted as a part of the Barclay's loan approval process. They didn't have the money. The $700,000,000 from the special dividend barely moved Lennar's net cash balances and in fact may have averted insolvency in the first quarter of 2007. Lennar had no available cash to buy land in 2007. In fact, before the end of the year, they were selling land assets wholesale, taking large losses, and applying for huge tax refunds.

Even their sister company LNR eventually was flirting with bankruptcy, and in fact went so far as to retain bankruptcy counsel.

The built-in conflicts of interest in this situation were astounding:

- Lennar was the manager of LandSource.
- Lennar was the projected buyer of 70% or more of the anticipated property sales by LandSource, along with LNR.
- Lennar provided the crucial information to prepare cash flow projections and the appraisal data used to place the 1.4 billion dollar loan from Barclay's loan syndicate.
- Lennar restructured LandSource to obtain valuable collateral from CALPERS to use to obtain the loan. Lennar implemented the special dividend used to remove all but a token amount of cash from the LandSource balance sheet at the worst possible time.
- Lennar managed the entities looted to provide enough cash to avoid the all-important bankruptcy preference period.
- Lennar orchestrated the LandSource bankruptcy filing in Delaware and masterminded the entire pennies-on-the-dollar repurchase process.
- Lennar ended up, through the bankruptcy process, with partial ownership and full control of LandSource's assets for a small fraction of the fraudulently obtained "special dividend." And control means control of the checkbook, and we know what that means.

• Lennar might argue that they "reduced" or "gave up" a portion of their ownership in LandSource in conjunction with the Calpers/Barclays transaction, but so what? The special dividend sucked out most of the equity in Land-Source anyway, so Lennar's reduction in ownership was like giving up their deck chair on the *Titanic*.

ONE OF THE unexplained aspects of this swindle is the question of why didn't CALPERS react swiftly to a loss of almost $1,000,000,000 in cash and valuable assets and demand that Lennar either support LandSource, put back the special dividend, or make CALPERS whole. It was abundantly clear that Lennar and LNR didn't follow through on the representations made to Barclays Bank to induce them to loan. The deal was in trouble within mere weeks of funding the "special dividend."

Miller appeared on CNBC on January 9, 2009, and claimed, when questioned about the validity of the Land-Source deal, that "That deal (LandSource) has been "vetted" both in the press and it's been looked at pretty carefully." Oh, really? How did the press "vet" fraudulent appraisals and cooked-up cash flow projections? Did Lennar share them with the press? Who looked at it carefully? Obviously not CALPERS.

But why not? There were more red flags flying here than a Chinese May Day parade.

Weren't all of the collateralized mortgage obligations and bonds cooked up on Wall Street that have unraveled amidst proven fraud allegations "vetted?" CitiCorp and

Bank of America alone have paid out over $20 billion dollars in fines and penalties for creating and selling those types of financial instruments. Especially the vetted ones.

And speaking of, in Miller's terms, "vetted by the press":

Headlines screamed in August of 2010 that CALPERS had been defrauded by Lennar and its sister company. For example, the *Sacramento Bee* wrote:

CALPERS Defrauded in $922 Million LandSource Deal

So it was true that the *Bee* vetted the transaction. The *Bee* quoted the well-researched unsecured creditors lawsuit and noted that "LandSource painted a fraudulent picture of its corporate health."

CALPERS responded by claiming that *"It was decided that the prudent decision was that we just cut our loss and move on."* How would you "cut your loss" by moving on? "Moving on" guaranteed the loss. They were already fully invested. But move on they did, even though the unsecured creditor's suit filed by then did the heavy lifting in regard to an accurate analysis of exactly how Jaffe and Lennar pulled off this caper.

And so 1.6 million participants in CALPERS collectively lost nearly $1,000,000,000 at the hands of Lennar. And the question still remained: why didn't CALPERS respond to the painfully obvious fact that they were defrauded by Lennar?

The following headline appeared on May 18, 2010:

CALPERS In Dire Straits Following Huge Investment Losses, Asks For $600 Million In Funding From Bankrupt California

CALPERS requested that the state of California contribute an additional $600,000,000 to CALPERS to cover *"huge investment losses."* Six Hundred Million! A lot of money, but less than the Lennar theft. Dire Straits.

So, losing almost a billion dollars is no big deal one day, and the next day the California taxpayers are being asked to foot the bill for *"huge investment losses?"* In a state where Governor Schwarzenegger, aka The Terminator, is coping with a 20 billion dollar shortfall! So now, in addition to Lennar fleecing the participants in the CALPERS retirement fund, California taxpayers are now being asked to foot the bill for $600,000,000. Something smells here, and it is the stench emanating from Lennar, its executives, and their odious schemes.

And it gets better: (or worse, depending on your perspective) — CALPERS is now in a no-holds-barred legal confrontation with at least two bankrupt California cities, Stockton and San Bernardino, and at least one municipal bond fund over prioritization of pension contributions to CALPERS. The claimed amounts at stake range from $7,000,000 to around $30,000,000. These amounts aren't small, but are nothing compared to Lennar's heist of nearly a billion dollars.

CALPERS might argue they are fighting so vociferously

and expensively to avoid an adverse ruling or precedent, but even if they win, the numbers are pennies compared to what they have to make up as a result of the loss of a billion dollars.

Can you imagine any well-managed hedge fund or lender in the country leaving a billion dollars on the table under these conditions and *"moving on"* instead of pursuing Lennar to the ends of the earth? If a hedgie like Paul Singer (Don't cry for me, Argentina) was swindled by Lennar, the Lennar executives would never have to get a dictionary out and look up the words "pursuit" "persistence", and "pay me." Here is a perfect real-world example:

This is a series of quotes from a March 2014 *Forbes* article concerning a "fraud in the inducement" lawsuit filed in connection with the reorganization of Quiznos. Ironically, the suit was filed in the same Delaware bankruptcy court where LandSource was filed by Lennar:

> *"Over the past nine months, the company said, it has conducted an investigation "regarding alleged misconduct that arose in connection with the 2012 restructuring" that revealed that certain of the company's former managers, owners and directors engaged in "a concerted effort to deceive other members of the debtors management, certain minority board members, and the debtors then-existing lenders."*

More specifically the company said its investigation revealed that internal financial projections and related projections "demonstrate that the financial projections created . . . and provided to the debtors then-existing lenders in connection with the 2012 restructuring were not reasonable and gave the false impression that after the 2012 restructuring the debtors could service their debt obligations and sustain their new capital structure."

The investigation revealed that the company's senior managers knew in 2011 that a substantial discrepancy existed . . . and based the projections provided to the debtors then existing lenders on the model that contained inaccurate and inflated data.

This case could not be more on point except for one thing: the claims in this case are for "only" hundreds of millions — a far less amount than Lennar defrauded the participants in the LandSource swindle.

"Moving on" and *"cut your loss"* isn't a valid explanation by CALPERS executives. No meaningful investigation or explanation of why the LandSource deal unraveled immediately after funding the special dividend had occurred. So what was the real explanation?

The answer may have come in a series of bombshell disclosures regarding the governance of CALPERS — a pay-to-play environment rife with bribery, payoffs, and a justice department investigation. Indictments of top CALPERS officials came down in March of 2013.

And in a stunning turn of events on July 11, 2014, Fred Buenrostro, the CEO of CALPERS, pled guilty to bribery, conspiracy, and depriving the citizens of the State of California of honest services.

Included in the plea was this statement by Mr. Buenrostro:

> *"As CEO, the highest ranking officer with powers and duties from the CALPERS Board of Administration, I was responsible for, among other things, the administration of CALPERS' financial affairs, including the operation of CALPERS investment staff and was entrusted with, among other things, confidential, internal, and proprietary information relating to CALPERS ongoing investments and prospective investment decisions in connection with CALPERS' administration of billions of dollars in assets."*

And read this stunning revelation:

> *"By the end of approximately 2007, Villalobos had made, and I had ac-*

cepted, bribes totaling approximately $200,000 in cash, all of which was delivered directly to me in the Hyatt hotel in downtown Sacramento across from the Capitol. Villalobos delivered the first two payments of approximately $50,000 each in a paper bag, while the last installment of approximately $100,000 was delivered in a shoebox."

There is little doubt that Mr. Buenrostro would have had to review and approve the Lennar/CALPERS/Barclays/LandSource transaction, and even less doubt that he had the final authority to make the decision on behalf of CALPERS to either demand an unwinding of the clearly fraudulent transaction or to "*move on*" and "*cut your loss.*" He was CEO. The buck stopped there.

And since the *Sacramento Bee*, Mr. Buenrostro's hometown newspaper, had published headlines screaming **CALPERS Defrauded In $922 Million LandSource Deal**, he certainly knew or should have known that there was something seriously wrong with the LandSource transaction.

So $200,000 in cash and a few perks were enough to wreck his career, go to jail, perhaps lose his pension, but $922 million is no big deal? If you put $922 million dollars in paper bags and shoeboxes it would take a lot more that a Hyatt Hotel room to hold it all.

Another rotten-to-the-core CEO! There appears to be no statute of limitations barring claims for defrauding a public entity like CALPERS, so who knows what the future may bring for Mr. Miller, Mr. Jaffe, and their little helpers?

The discovery of the LandSource scheme, the discovery of the looting of our jointly-owned venture, and the exposure of other wrongdoing by Lennar and its executives heightened Stuart Miller's obsession with discrediting the message and the messenger and has fueled a Lennar litigation vendetta that has continued unabated to this day. Which takes us to . . .

CHAPTER NINE

Litigation Vendetta

LITIGATION WITH LENNAR commenced at the start of 2007 after all efforts failed to reach an agreement over Bridges accounting issues and other legitimate disputes.

As previously mentioned, Lennar's curious choice for lead lawyer in the cases was Daniel Petrocelli of the O'Melveny & Myers firm in Los Angeles. He has had an interesting career. He is an unpleasant little man with a gift for lying convincingly to just about anybody willing to listen.

He first achieved some recognition while representing the Ron Goldman family in Los Angeles in a wrongful death action against O.J. Simpson. Petrocelli won the case. But the measure of success in a civil case is usually monetary, and unfortunately the Goldman family has collected almost nothing, and never will. Mr. Simpson was viewed as guilty by all but about twelve (you know which twelve) of the three hundred million or so people living in the United States. So, with a much lower burden of proof in the civil litigation environment than in a criminal trial, and with a trial held in West

LA, notching a win on the Goldman case couldn't have been too difficult.

Petrocelli's next high-profile case was a disastrous criminal defense of CEO Jeffrey Skilling over the collapse of Enron. The trial was in Houston. At the conclusion of one of the most expensive trials in history, Mr. Skilling was sentenced to 25 years in jail and fined over $50,000,000. He is still in jail.

There are remarkable parallels in this story between Mr. Petrocelli's clients, Stuart Miller and Jeffrey Skilling, and their companies, Lennar and Enron.

Mr. Skilling is a Harvard graduate as is Mr. Miller. It is notable that both of Petrocelli's Harvard-educated clients hold the all-time records for defrauding California residents.

Enron Corp, with Skilling as CEO, willfully defrauded California utility customers out of over $9,000,000,000 in a well-documented scheme tied to an Enron-promoted deregulation of the California utility market. Enron's deregulation ploy even forced giant Pacific Gas & Electric into bankruptcy.

Enron traders even had names for the various schemes concocted to defraud California utilities and their customers: Donkey Punch, Ping Pong, Russian Roulette, Big and Little Tuna, Sidewinder, Little Man etc.

But Petrocelli, in his closing arguments to the jury in Houston described Enron as a "Wonderful Company" and a "Shining Star." The jury didn't agree.

LENNAR, WITH STUART Miller as CEO, cheated CALPERS and its 1.6 million participants out of nearly a billion dollars, and caused CALPERS to seek $600,000,000 from the already overburdened California taxpayers to cover the loss. Maybe Miller copied Skilling's homework at Harvard.

Pity the unfortunate CALPERS pensioners caught in the middle: one Petrocelli client was picking their pockets through their utility bills and another Petrocelli client was hijacking their pensions. Wonderful Companies? Shining Stars? Not Exactly!

Petrocelli will stop at nothing, legal or illegal, on behalf of his clients. He has lied repeatedly orally and in writing to triers-of-fact in various venues during the litigation process with us, and coached the Lennar executives to do the same.

In the Florida case, he actually lied to and misled jurors and in the process undermined the very jury system we depend on in this country. And he co-opted a judge to help him do it. He has lied repeatedly in courtrooms from Florida to California to aid and abet his clients' theft of millions of dollars from me and my company.

Petrocelli was described as "silver-tongued" in the definitive book on the Enron collapse, *The Smartest Guys in the Room* by Bethany McClain and Peter Elkind. He is most certainly that. But don't confuse silver tongued with truthful. He has an amazing ability to look a judge right in the eye and lie with consummate skill. He is the go-to lawyer for corporate wrong-doers, and will stop at nothing to get them off the hook. And that is why he, of all the available attorneys in the country, was hired by Lennar.

The essence of magic is to get someone to look in the

wrong place at the right time. And Petrocelli is entitled to credit where credit is due. He has developed the ability to fool, distract, misdirect, fabricate evidentiary issues, blow smoke, shine mirrors, and create an alternate universe where his clients are paragons of virtue and the other side is reprehensible in every way.

He is the lawyer you hire if you did it — but don't want to settle, pay, get caught, or worse, convicted. It is no coincidence that Miller hired Petrocelli. He defends the indefensible. For a price.

Petrocelli's history representing Jeffrey Skilling is instructive. Published reports indicate that Petrocelli's firm billed Jeffrey Skilling a sum in excess of $70,000,000 in a criminal defense of charges including fraud, conspiracy, and insider trading. But despite Petrocelli's best efforts, Mr. Skilling was convicted, jailed, fined, and all of his assets were tied up or impounded by the government.

Billing is one thing, collecting is another, as many law firms have painfully realized during this prolonged downturn. News reports, including MSNBC on October 23, 2006, indicated that Mr. Petrocelli's law firm received $40,000,000 from a combination of $23,000,000 from Skilling's bank account and an additional $17,000,000 from various insurance companies. But Mr. Petrocelli and his firm billed Mr. Skilling over $70,000,000, leaving an unpaid bill of over $30,000,000.

So at the conclusion of the trial, Petrocelli and his team had to pack up and leave Houston with their tails between their legs. And they were in the hole over $30,000,000 dollars. Essentially that meant that $30,000,000 of his firm's resources were tied up and not earning revenue for the firm during the duration of the Skilling trial.

With their client hauled off to jail, and Skilling's assets frozen by the government, no further cash was available to pay legal fees and costs. Petrocelli had some "splainin" to do when he got back to the office in Los Angeles, and a deep hole to fill.

A $30,000,000 revenue loss had to be replaced by Petrocelli's firm, which is not so easy. A three to five million a year law firm client is considered a whale using Las Vegas parlance. How many clients are out there that are both willing and capable of arranging and spending in excess of $70,000,000 in legal fees? Not too many. Where could they find a new goat to milk for that kind of money? Had to be a big one! In just a matter of a few months after the Skilling debacle, they had the answer: Lennar.

Hello, Stuart Miller! It is estimated that, to date, Lennar has expended well in excess of $100,000,000 of shareholder money and company resources on litigation costs, expenses, and executive and management personnel costs on its insane litigation vendetta. And no doubt more litigation and more squandered shareholder money is yet to come.

A river of cash has flowed into Mr. Petrocelli's firm, and the rest of the money into five or more California and Florida law firms retained by Lennar. Petrocelli instantly figured out that Miller was the perfect target. Miller is vain, arrogant, self-impressed, and egocentric. He is an individual who clearly has no moral compass and has been complicit in defrauding Lennar partners, lenders, suppliers, and others.

And it is axiomatic that dishonest clients need and require unethical lawyers.

Most importantly, CEO Stuart Miller was clearly willing to squander Lennar shareholder money on a win-at-all-costs legal battle designed to discredit and silence a defrauded partner instead of simply pursuing a business solution to a business problem.

Upon retention by Lennar, Mr. Petrocelli re-assembled essentially the entire team of lawyers, paralegals, and support staff that had been transferred to Houston for the Skilling trial. Lennar then hired additional law firms in California, and two more law firms in Florida, the home team.

Contrast this: The Skilling case was all about federal prosecutors — aka the United States of America — versus Mr. Skilling. The stakes were very high, and the opponent the most formidable on the planet.

Did the case of "where's the money?" in a development deal and a "deal-steal" case in Rancho Santa Fe, California really require the same team plus additional law firms coast to coast?

Costlier than Skillings' failed defense? By far? Unlikely, seeing as we had just a few lawyers, reasonable and well-grounded claims, and my consistently stated interest was to simply resolve the matter without expensive and time-consuming litigation.

In fact, the answer to the question of whether or not Lennar needed a coast-to-coast battalion of lawyers with an unlimited budget to defend against our claims is categorically no — unless there is something else that had Miller and Jaffe very, very concerned. Even more striking is this: Jeffrey Skilling didn't have a choice: he was up against the United States of America, and he was in survival mode.

But Miller and Lennar had a choice, yet they made decisions that resulted in legal and corporate expenditures far exceeding Skilling's stratospheric fees and costs. Why is that?

Petrocelli's first official act upon his involvement in the litigation process on behalf of Lennar was to cancel a scheduled mediation of our claims that may well have resulted in an equitable settlement.

His second official act was to begin the name-calling, labelling, character assassination and subversion of the legal process that are his trademark approach to litigation. Thinking much like a clinical pathological liar, he created an alternate universe where his clients are victims. Then he manufactured evidentiary issues to divert the courts' attention from the basic allegations in the cases. Petrocelli spent millions of dollars of Lennar shareholder money to assert false claims and paint my company in a bad light regardless of the meritless alternate universe theory or the fabricated evidentiary claims.

Every opposing witness in the Skilling — Enron trial was depicted by Petrocelli as a "liar," "crook" and "conspirator," his usual method of operation. My company and I were about to experience the same tactics.

Petrocelli's motives doing Lennar's dirty work were easily understood: it takes buckets of constant recurring cash flow to run a law firm like O'Melveny & Myers. Settling cases does not pay the bills. Self-aggrandizement doesn't come cheap either (another Petrocelli trait). He also was just coming off an expensive divorce, a big loss in Houston, had a big deficit to make up, and needed to prove he wasn't washed up.

Maybe with enough resources available Petrocelli could shore up his reputation and bank balances by beating up and overwhelming just one of hundreds of Lennar joint venture partners. He would still require the help of the estimated 15 or more California lawyers assigned to the case plus ten or more lawyers in Florida. And unlimited funding from Lennar.

Miller's motives were less clear. Yes, he is a self-impressed guy with a perpetual smirk on his face who can and has squandered Lennar shareholder money and corporate assets to fund a long-running legal vendetta designed to discredit and overwhelm another Lennar fraud victim, but to prove what?

That Lennar and its lawyers can subvert and abuse the legal process and beat up a partner in a successful development for daring to ask where the venture's money was going?

You might be right if you think that, but there was much, much, more driving Stuart Miller and Jaffe. It was certainly no coincidence that Miller found a lawyer well versed in defending corporate wrong-doers and criminals.

Stuart Miller and Daniel Petrocelli established an immediate rapport. It was love at first sight! Miller got a lawyer willing to defend some of the most egregious corporate behavior in the country — he already had in the Enron case! And Petrocelli found a goat to milk for the foreseeable future! Miller had unfettered access to Lennar's bank accounts and shareholder money without board oversight, governance, or restraint. Ka-Ching!

To prove how out of the ordinary this situation had become, it is instructive to read Stuart Miller's own testimony about the expenditures in this case versus any legal case Lennar had undertaken in its entire history:

In a deposition taken on May 23, 2012, Mr. Miller testified:

Q. Do you have a sense for the aggregate amount of money that has been spent by Lennar in its disputes with Mr. Marsch since the first time you spent a dollar on that issue?

A. I don't really know the number, but let's say in excess of $50,000,000.

Even more questions arise when this litigation process is examined in the context of Lennar Corp's general litigation history according to Stuart Miller. In a deposition taken on May 24, 2012 Mr. Miller testified:

Q. Do you have a sense as to what your average case costs, as a general matter, roughly speaking?

A. Probably — I would say our average case probably costs, you know, under $50—or $100,000, I would guess.

Q. Do you have a sense of what the average complex case costs?

A. No, but it would be materially more.

Q. A million dollars more, or does your average case cost less than a million dollars?

A. Maybe.

Q. Does Lennar have a lot of litigations where they spend more than seven figures on legal fees?

A. No. I would say very, very, very, few.

Petrocelli and his firm were definitely not hired to simply produce the long-promised but withheld accounting numbers, to engage in a straight-forward defense of the claims, or even to try to reach an equitable resolution. In fact, Mr. Petrocelli was employed because his particular skill set is a scorched-earth approach to litigation which includes but is not limited to:

Character Assassination and Media Smear Campaigns. He and his firm engage in name-calling, labeling, and reputational destruction. The firm hires top media spin companies to prepare and disseminate defamatory press releases designed to impugn and destroy the reputation of whomever they target. Petrocelli participates in this as well.

Resource Exhaustion and Abuse of Process. Perhaps the primary tool employed by Mr. Petrocelli and his associates is to engage in a gross abuse of the legal process, including but not limited to filing endless claims and lawsuits, scheduling and taking prolonged depositions, making extensive document demands, mischaracterizing testimony obtained in depositions in court filings, and the filing of mile-high motions on every possible issue. Forget about our country's rule of law and due process when these lawyers are involved.

Fabricated Evidentiary Issues. This is also a primary tool of Mr. Petrocelli. The goal is to limit or prevent the other side from defending against the endless litigation onslaught by the Petrocelli team, drawing the court's attention away from the primary issues in the case, and above all, painting the other side in a bad light. Suddenly the plaintiffs are the villains, and his clients are either blameless or actually victims. The alternate universe.

Attacking Opposing Counsel. They attack and try to disqualify opposing counsel, and if that fails, they spend enough money to discourage and intimidate them in an effort to cause a withdrawal or force a quick settlement.

Co-opting Judges. We have witnessed inexplicable and inexcusable behavior by judges as soon as Petrocelli got involved in a case. In San Diego, for example, the judge allowed overt coaching of Lennar witnesses, did nothing about it, and then made adverse rulings using the tainted evidence. And read Chapter 16 of this book to see the ultimate example of this behavior.

And the beauty of these tactics is that they unduly enrich his law firm at the expense of their clients.

I have been in courtrooms where the Lennar legal team has fielded up to 14 lawyers. Some watched, some participated, all billed. Many took turns objecting, name calling, talking, arguing, and it was all designed to overwhelm the plaintiff and overworked or gullible judges. In the courtroom it sounded at times like a Greek chorus in an echo chamber! Objection! Objection! Objection! Liar! Liar! Liar!

The fact that these techniques work so well exposes a major flaw in our legal system. If it is simply a matter of who brings the most money to a legitimate business dispute and hires the most competent liars, then they should take down the sign on the court house that reads "Hall of Justice" and just replace it with a dollar sign, or change the sign to read "Justice For Sale To The Highest Bidder."

Petrocelli tried these techniques in Houston for Mr. Skilling, but it's not easy to outspend or outshout the U.S. Government. For one thing, the government can actually print money. Legally!

In an epilogue to the definitive book on the Enron collapse, *The Smartest Guys in the Room,* the authors described

Petrocelli as a "Hired Gun" and recounted the endless stream of pre-trial motions generated by Petrocelli and his team. Right out of the playbook.

Research shows that Petrocelli and his well-trained legal goon squad used this scorched-earth approach or variations thereof in lawsuits filed on behalf of clients throughout the country. Sometimes these tactics work, but sometimes Petrocelli's clients end up financially impaired or even in jail. But his firm wins almost every time.

In reviewing cases involving Mr. Petrocelli across the country at least one pattern emerges clearly. He and his team fabricate or trump up even minor or in many cases non-existent evidentiary issues into accusations of intentional evidence mishandling that are designed to both draw the court's attention away from the basic issues presented to the court for adjudication and to paint the other side in a bad light. The ultimate goal is to convince the court to set aside due process, constitutional rights, and to take away the other side's right to defend the case. This actually happened to us.

In one recently reported case in Los Angeles involving a dispute over the movie *The Last Samurai*, Mr. Petrocelli and his associates surreptitiously obtained illegal DNA samples of a deponent and his lawyer by inviting them to lunch at the O'Melveny & Myers Los Angeles offices in the guise of a "settlement" discussion, then retrieved cups and utensils, took DNA samples of the deponent and his lawyer to use as "evidence" in an ongoing proceeding involving Warner Brothers. Opposing counsel was justifiably outraged and sought fines and imprisonment for Mr. Petrocelli and his associates. "Win-at-all-costs" is the rule of the day, but truth and fair play are not.

By the end of 2008 Lennar had filed even more lawsuits and counterclaims in California and Florida against my company and me in a coast to coast effort to overwhelm, submerge, and discourage us with litigation costs. The classic resource exhaustion technique. And it works.

The two cases filed by us in San Diego in connection with claims arising from the Bridges development were assigned to a San Diego superior court judge. The judge proved to be no match for the O'Melveny legal team and the overwhelming torrent of procedural motions, character assassination, lies, attacks on opposing counsel, and fabricated evidentiary issues propounded by Mr. Petrocelli and his team.

The average case load of a Superior Court judge in San Diego is over 700 cases. What judge could realistically keep up with the torrent of motions filed by a law firm like Petrocelli's operating on an unlimited budget from Lennar?

The judge quickly succumbed to Petrocelli's tactics of overwhelming procedural abuse and lies. He began rubber-stamping or acquiescing to just about anything the Petrocelli team asked for. Motions served in the process were often two to three feet thick.

Speaking of resource exhaustion tactics, when time came for the Bridges trial, Lennar authorized and paid for renting 5,000 sq. ft. of office space across from the courthouse and 20 suites in the Westin hotel downtown. This was to house and provide office space for 28 lawyers, paralegals, and support staff.

This too is reminiscent of the Skilling trial. As recounted in the epilogue:

"Days before jury selection, he (Skilling) and Petrocelli launched their own PR offensive, granting a string of media interviews during which they led reporters through the suite of offices the defense team had leased across the street from the federal courthouse in downtown Houston."

Although Petrocelli and his team provided a two month trial estimate to the Bridges trial judge, it was clear from the beginning this was no two month trial they were setting up to conduct. It was going to be a textbook resource exhaustion and siege process.

We had two lawyers and a small support staff for the Bridges case. All of them capable, honest, and hard working, but they were in for the ride of their lives. In retrospect, Custer had a better chance at Little Big Horn. There were sometimes up to ten lawyers in the court room representing Lennar. And they had more parked across the street. And yet more in offices from Orange County to Los Angeles and San Francisco. And Miami.

The trial judge, at the urging of Petrocelli, failed to call a jury even though a jury trial was demanded, and announced he would try the case himself. He then ceded control of the trial and the schedule to the O'Melveny firm and what then occurred set all records for gross abuse of process. Endless motions, endless objections, endless hearings, witness coaching and tampering, and a blatant effort to exhaust our resources and simply outspend and outwait us.

After a trial lasting more than eleven months (so much for the "two month" trial estimate), the judge signed an order that was crafted almost entirely by Mr. Petrocelli and his associates and that essentially ignored or threw out all of the written documents (in a business deal!) and instead accepted tainted oral evidence (not even admissible) from the coached Lennar executives and made-up facts which were used as a basis for a one-sided and punitive decision.

It has been our experience in this coast to coast litigation process with Lennar and its lawyers that, in most cases, the judges quickly fell prey to the overwhelming procedural abuse tactics employed by Petrocelli. They rapidly succumbed to the moving vans full of motions and documents endlessly filed with the court. The motions that were invariably filled with nonstop invective and outright lies. Then the tedious hearings and arguments following these motions sealed the deal, and the judges began signing virtually anything put in front of them.

To have a situation where judges routinely sign submitted orders without review or change is viewed by the general legal community as an abandonment of the basic duties entrusted to the court. But that is exactly what happened.

No better example of this was the series of punitive orders that were submitted by Lennar's lawyers to Florida judges and signed without change. This process is described in detail in Chapter 16. The word "compliant" would not be adequate to describe the Florida judges responsible for signing these egregious orders.

So, few plaintiffs or defendants, their counsel, and very few judges are prepared for the overwhelming and extraordinarily well-funded litigation tactics employed by Mr. Petrocelli and his team. All funded by unwitting Lennar shareholders. The overwhelming litigation onslaught was taking its toll (that was the idea) and we needed something or someone to help level the playing field. And that is exactly what happened.

CHAPTER TEN

The Whistleblower Letter

AS MENTIONED EARLIER in this book, an anonymous but highly credible whistleblower letter was mailed to my office in November 2008 regarding Lennar's dishonest business practices. The postmark was just a few miles from Lennar's Southern California headquarters.

Whistleblowers have played an indispensable role in at least two recent cases, exposing the largest and most egregious fraudulent and criminal activity in modern times. These cases are the Enron fraud, and the Madoff Ponzi scheme.

Enron's downfall started with an anonymous whistleblower letter written by an Enron employee and sent directly to Enron's chairman, Kenneth Lay.

Bernie Madoff's date with the FBI came when his own sons turned him in. The rest is history.

In both cases, these whistleblowers were uniquely positioned to witness or discover criminal conduct. The Enron whistleblower was ultimately identified as an Enron employee named Sherron Watkins, who was the Vice President of Corporate Development. Ms. Watkins had access to certain internal Enron documents and knew exactly what she was seeing. And correctly predicted the outcome if this fraudulent behavior came to light. And it did. Her predictions came true. Enron is history.

But she started out with an *anonymous* letter to the chairman of Enron, Kenneth Lay. Some whistleblowers are certainly in it for the money, but many whistleblowers have a conscience and are deeply offended by the fraudulent and criminal behavior they witness far too often in corporate America. And that described Ms. Watkins perfectly.

To underscore the important role whistleblowers have played recently in exposing corporate fraud and criminal activity, three prominent whistleblowers were featured in 2002 on the cover of *Time* magazine as "Persons of the Year." And Ms. Watkins was among the three. In describing these whistleblowers, *Time* said "All three are just resolute and standing up for what is right."

Much like the Enron whistleblower, the Lennar whistleblower was offended by Lennar's dishonest business practices.

ON-LINE POSTINGS REVEAL that there are very large numbers of ex-Lennar employees who view the company as a corporate criminal, and its executives as thoroughly dishonest. And they instill fear in their employees:

"To work in fear of any kind of retribution . . . is emotionally and mentally devastating."

"Ever since I wrote an email to the CEO of Lennar my work life has spiraled downhill. Oh, by the way, I work for Lennar."

THE LENNAR WHISTLEBLOWER was clearly a Lennar upper management-level employee in Southern California. He or she was positioned to observe a pattern of fraudulent and criminal conduct by top Lennar executives, including Stuart Miller, Jon Jaffe, and others. And was positioned much as Sherron Watkins was at Enron's headquarters in Houston.

The letter I received was postmarked just a few miles from Lennar's Southern California Aliso Viejo offices. It was clear from the letter that the writer was well positioned in the company to provide accurate inside information on Lennar's illegal activities. The letter starts:

"I am aware you are seeking legal action against Lennar for improper management relating to your joint venture. As a manager, I have witnessed endless improprieties made by Stuart Miller, Jon Jaffe and management.

Note that the author of the letter points directly to Miller, Jaffe, and management, not some low level rogue employees. The stench emanating from this company starts at the top and permeates the culture of the company. The letter goes on to say:

"I have been involved in unwinding all of material Lennar off-balance sheet joint ventures. I have been instructed to move everything

back on to the balance sheet as quickly as possible to avoid further in-
quiries from either the FBI or the SEC Enforcement Agency."

By the way, note that this comment comes well before the FDI Red Flags Report published the following January on that exact issue. One thing was clear from the letter: Lennar was furiously unwinding their off-balance sheet joint ventures one step ahead of the authorities.

The letter also continuously referred to ongoing inquiries by the SEC and the FBI into Lennar's business practices and alluded to the fact that Lennar was moving assets around in a shell game to deceive regulatory and law enforcement agencies, shareholders, Wall Street analysts, and credit rating agencies. The letter states:

"I can guarantee Stuart Miller, Jon Jaffe and management are extremely sensitive to this matter. Guess what; I would be afraid of going to jail too."

The letter then goes on to describe in very specific details how Miller was using the company to enrich himself and his friends at the company's expense. Including his friend and neighbor the basketball player Rony Seikely. This information tied precisely with information we learned independently from the litigation discovery process. And that went a long way toward validating the contents of the rest of the letter.

I had provided the letter to FDI in the quest to locate the author. Then, shortly thereafter, Lennar and Miller became aware of the existence of the whistleblower letter when FDI published its Red Flags Report on January 9, 2009.

Suddenly Stuart Miller had to deal with two problems simultaneously: A way-too-well-informed anonymous inside whistleblower *and* FDI, a recognized outside whistleblower. Two whistles blowing at the same can make a lot of noise. Especially if the whistleblowers knew what they are talking about. And that is why Miller may have needed an underwear change to get ready for the CNBC interview later that day.

Lennar released an initial written response to the Red Flags Report on January 12, 2009. The response was directed in part to the anonymous letter and included some absolute nonsense about the "confidential" procedures available within the company to whistleblowers.

Here is what the press release said:

"Lennar has extensive confidential procedures in place to ensure the free flow of communications by whistleblowers and to ensure their protection from retaliation."

Those confidential procedures, on a practical basis, created a mechanism that resulted in information that came from a whistleblower to end up in one or both of two places: either the Lennar board, or Lennar's senior management.

Let's look at either option from an inside and very knowledgeable whistleblower's viewpoint, and the likelihood of any communications to senior management or the board remaining confidential:

Option 1 — Directing the contents of the letter to senior management. This option would be out of the question because the letter specifically implicated Miller and Jaffe in criminal behavior. Given the atmosphere of fear throughout the company, and the gravity of the charges, a whistleblower would have more than justifiable fears for his or her own personal safety. And no protection from retaliation.

Option 2 — Directing the contents of the letter to the Board of Directors. Not a good choice either. Miller is on the board. Nothing would prevent Miller from immediate access to the letter. Again, no protection from retaliation.

Plus, the whistleblower observed that Miller was routinely directing Lennar to enrich and favor his friends at the expense of Lennar shareholders. The letter stated:

> *"Mr. Miller ordered us to pay back Mr. Seikely and his company their principal on three other joint ventures. These four joint ventures are projected to incur significant losses and Mr. Miller chose to have Lennar's shareholders take the losses, not Mr. Seikely. Another example is the Playa Vista joint venture. This also included Mr. Miller's friend where the company had to return their principal investment. Why he didn't require them to take their prorate share of the loss is harming and upsetting."*

So the whistleblower could obviously see two things: one, that Miller was on the board, therefore so much for confidentiality and "protection from retaliation." And, two, that the Board was either unaware that Miller was using company resources to enrich his friends, or the Board was so under Miller's thumb that, either way, the likely response to a direct non-anonymous communication to either senior management or the board would elicit a "kill the messenger" response.

Look at my experience with the Board. I wrote a letter, and was sued within days. And *"protection from retaliation?"* Get serious. I have experienced threats to myself and my family, illegal surveillance, thugs beating on our doors, phone hacking, an unprecedented and relentless legal onslaught, and an overwhelming effort to silence me, ruin my reputation, and destroy my life.

This whistleblower letter, in combination with the FDI Red Flags Report, spelled Trouble with a capital T for Lennar and its top executives. And they knew it.

To this day we do not know who wrote the letter, but we do know this: Miller, Jaffe, and Lennar's in-house general counsel, Mark Sustana most likely know exactly who wrote the letter. And the Lennar Board may know, as well.

Here is some revealing testimony from these three key Lennar executives taken in 2012. Observe the striking differences in testimony by Mr. Miller, Mr. Sustana, and Mr. Jaffe while answering under oath the same questions regarding Lennar's efforts to identify the author of the whistleblower letter:

In a deposition taken on August 1, 2012 Mr. Sustana,

in-house general counsel for Lennar who offices directly with Mr. Miller, testified under oath:

Q. Was an investigation undertaken to identify the whistleblower?

A. We never had sufficient facts about Mr. Marsch's claimed whistleblower to even begin such an investigation.

Q. Did this letter trigger any internal investigation?

A. No. It wasn't sent to us, so I don't remember when we received it, but whenever we did, it did not trigger an investigation.

Q. Were you able to identify the author — Have you ever identified the author of this letter?

A. No.

Q. Was this letter shared with the board of directors?

A. I don't recall ever sharing this with the board. No.

Q. Has anyone identified the author of this letter?

A. No one that I know of.

But on May 24, 2012 in a deposition of Stuart Miller on the same exact topic, Mr. Miller testified quite differently under oath:

Q. Did Lennar ever conduct any kind of investigation to determine whether or not this document (the letter) was legitimate?

A. The answer is, yes. I — I believe that we made every attempt to try to figure out where this letter came from, who might have authored it . . . so the answer is, we spent — we spent a lot of time on this letter, trying to figure out whether it was real or anything else. And I didn't personally spend time on it, but Mark Sustana and our legal group did.

Q. At some point was there an outcome to the investigation?

A. I don't — I don't recall, but — let me say yes.

Q. And do you recall whether that outcome was conveyed to you verbally or in writing?

A. To me, verbally.

Q. — the outcome of that investigation? You said to you, verbally.

A. I don't recall.

Q. Were Lennar employees in California interviewed in connection with that investigation?

A. I believe they were.

Q. Approximately how many employees?

A. I wouldn't know. Mr. Sustana would have taken that charge.

Q. I mean was it a broad investigation where you just asked everyone, or was there some focus to just asking people in a particular location or a particular function within the company?

A. To all of this, I would say that the — this kind of investigation would have been driven by Mark Sustana, counsel.

Mr. Jaffe also testified under oath in a deposition taken on August 13, 2012, and his story was materially different than that of both Sustana and Miller:

Q. Did you participate in any investigation concerning the whistleblower letter that Mr. Marsch identified?

A. I'm not sure.

Q. Do you have any recollection of what Lennar did to identify the drafter of that letter?

A. I know that Lennar's board hired counsel to look into these matters. I don't know what they did to investigate.

Q. Were you ever addressed by the outside counsel? Not what you talked about, mind you, but were you ever addressed regarding a whistleblower letter?

A. I was addressed by that independent counsel. I don't recall if I was specifically asked about the alleged whistleblower letter or not.

What is going on here? In the same time frame, three key Lennar executives were deposed under oath with regard to the efforts to locate the author of the whistleblower letter. They gave wildly divergent testimony on the same exact topic. Keep in mind that two of the deponents, Mr. Miller and Mr. Jaffe, were singled out by the letter writer as candidates for a jail cell. Whistleblowers have brought down bigger companies than Lennar, so it is rather unlikely Miller and Jaffe would not have a vital interest in identifying and silencing the writer.

Mr. Sustana said there was no investigation, and the matter was never brought to the attention of the board. Mr. Miller, who offices with and is in contact all day every day with Mr. Sustana, said that there was an extensive investigation, headed by Mr. Sustana, and included extensive interviews of employees in California. Mr. Jaffe said that the board undertook an investigation using outside counsel (precisely the opposite of Mr. Sustana's testimony), but didn't know what the board did to investigate even though Miller said *"we made every attempt to try to figure out where this letter came from"* and that Lennar employees in California were interviewed and that Mr. Sustana handled the investigation.

The testimony given under oath by these executives has no credibility whatsoever. Did they miss the rehearsals with Petrocelli? We now know that the independent counsel retained by the board to investigate the allegations in the whistleblower letter was none other than Petrocelli himself. Sounds a lot like Enron.

It is a certainty that at least two of the Lennar executives are lying, and most probably all three. None identify the author of the letter but none reveal the results of the investigations into the matter, either. They know who the author is and they are concealing the identity from us, the courts, the SEC, and other victims who are mentioned in the letter.

Why three wildly divergent stories on the same exact topic? Their depositions under oath collectively read like a comedy skit. Are they just concealing Miller's largesse to his personal friends with the company's assets, or is there a lot more to hide?

Lennar's Board of Directors, essentially a hand-stacked board appointed by Miller, could be referred to as the Board of Mushrooms (you know the joke — feed them bull — and keep them in the dark). The Board allegedly hired outside counsel to review the letter and investigate. What happened? Is there a report? What did it say? What is the identity, job description, and contact information of the letter writer?

I have been on Lennar's executive floor in their Aliso Viejo offices many times. Jon Jaffe and all key executives work on the same floor. And there were probably less than ten people at the responsibility level of the anonymous letter writer who described himself or herself as a "manager." And would have had access to the information detailed in the letter.

Just how long would it have taken to eliminate anyone

who would not have access to the information in the letter, and concentrate on the remaining candidates? Like, for example, who knew who Miller's friends were and who was getting special treatment at shareholder expense? Like who knew of the existence of simultaneous investigations by the FBI and the SEC, and had also witnessed *"countless abuse(s) and improper accounting treatment?*

It's not like Lennar breathlessly phoned the *Wall Street Journal*, the analysts, their pal at Bloomberg, and the shareholders to let them know there were federal investigations underway. In fact, that is exactly what they didn't do. So the number of managers in the southern California office that would not only be aware of the investigations, but would be reluctantly participating in a scheme to mislead the SEC, the FBI, the shareholders, the analysts, and the credit rating agencies was of necessity going to be a very short list.

Clearly the writer was someone with a conscience that we needed to talk to and who might help level the playing field given Lennar's overwhelming coast to coast litigation vendetta fueled by shareholder money and orchestrated by Mr. Petrocelli.

THERE IS AN eerie parallel here to the series of events leading to the collapse of Enron. When on August 15, 2001, an Enron employee sent an anonymous memo detailing massive accounting irregularities within the company to the CEO of Enron, Kenneth Lay, he, in turn, decided that it would be appropriate to hire an outside law firm to investigate.

The selected law firm, Vinson & Elkins, was already deeply involved with Enron, including with the very off-balance sheet entities that troubled Ms. Watkins. So, not surprisingly, the law firm did little if any investigation and opined that there were no problems. But there certainly were. As fraud-based accounting problems began to surface, massive write-downs were taken, Enron stock went into a steady decline, events snowballed, and the company filed bankruptcy by the end of 2001.

The Lennar Board appointed Petrocelli to investigate the whistleblower matter. Good luck with that. What were the chances of a legitimate disclosure of the identity of the letter writer, and a fair and honest evaluation of the whistleblower's observations and issues? None. Just like Enron.

Consider this: Petrocelli and his firm were appointed to seek out the identity of the whistleblower letter writer by the Board. The list of potential authors was short. This was not a formidable task. Lennar, at the direction of Miller, has squandered untold sums of Lennar shareholder money on Petrocelli's services. It is inconceivable that with all of these resources available, the writer's identity remains a mystery to Lennar.

It was of great importance to us to locate and talk with the writer of the letter. The playing field could have been leveled in a hurry with the kind of information clearly available to the writer of the letter. I had a head start in the process of locating that person, but one thing I couldn't do (unlike Lennar or Petrocelli) was interview the obvious candidates at Lennar's Aliso Viejo offices.

Who or what organization would be of help in locating

the writer of the letter? Asking Lennar would be futile. The letter writer specifically referred to the SEC and the FBI and ongoing inquiry into Lennar's perceived criminal activities, so a potential investigator's connections with those agencies would be important. Then a curious coincidence provided the answer to that question.

CHAPTER ELEVEN

Fraud Discovery Institute

ON NOVEMBER 14, 2008 I read an article in the *Wall Street Journal* regarding former bad-boy Barry Minkow and his company, the Fraud Discovery Institute, or FDI. It was clear that Mr. Minkow was making a comeback. He was making a name for himself working with regulatory and law enforcement agencies to help expose Ponzi schemes, false corporate resumes, and everything in between.

Clearly we needed to level the playing field with Lennar. Their resource exhaustion strategy was . . . exhausting our resources. We had a credible whistleblower letter, and finding the author of the anonymous letter would go a long way to doing just that.

I was curious whether FDI might be a candidate to locate the writer of the letter I had received since the letter heavily emphasized the fact that Lennar was scrambling to stay one step ahead of the SEC and the FBI, and that potential or actual criminal violations were occurring on a regular basis.

The Fraud Discovery Institute's founder, Barry Minkow, had been convicted of a financial fraud committed as a teenager and spent time in prison. At seventeen years old he took a company public that had essentially no assets or prospects. Dishonest to be sure, but not exactly stupid. He paid his price to society and, upon release, he began working with various government and law enforcement agencies including the SEC, the FBI, the IRS, and others to assist them in fraud detection and prosecution. He became an ordained minister, got married, adopted two children, and seemed to be well on his way to making the most of his second chance in life.

I have a personal belief in second chances. Our country was founded on second chances. Many citizens, who at one point or another got in trouble, have paid their dues, gotten a second chance, and then they often resume or go on to successful lives and become productive members of society. Even Martha Stewart spent a little time in Club Fed but is certainly back in business in a big way. And there is a long list of similar examples.

Mr. Minkow had quickly established himself as the "go to" guy for federal agencies charged with unraveling complex and difficult-to-prosecute fraudulent schemes. He certainly knew a fraudulent scheme when he saw one. He was instrumental in assisting various law enforcement agencies in identifying, charging, and prosecuting those engaged in all types of fraudulent activity. He won the praises of a wide range of regulatory and law enforcement agencies, financial institutions, and law firms. This included the FBI, the IRS, the SEC, and even the U.S. Army. He also was an in-demand speaker on the topic of fraud detection and prevention on college campuses, at law enforcement seminars, law firms, and other venues.

Here is just a small selection of quotes from numerous letters of commendation written to Mr. Minkow and FDI:

> *September 9, 1996 — FBI — "... Your presentation was very well received as evidenced by the course evaluations and personal comments made to me by many of the attendees. On behalf of the FBI and all of the attendees I want to express our sincere thanks for a job well done . . . "*

> *January 21, 2003 — City National Bank — I . . . will be recommending you to the person who is responsible for fraud detection within City National Bank and will encourage them to use you in our training sessions on the subject."*

> *March 8, 2004 — Department of Justice — ". . . Thank you again for your willingness to assist the FBI in its White Collar Crime training efforts. Your participation was invaluable to the success of this in-service training."*

And he was involved in providing useful and valuable training information to the U.S. Army's Internal Review community, as well.

> *"Dear Mr. Minkow:*
>
> *Thank you for your support at our recent Worldwide Army Internal Review Training Symposium . . . you provided the Army's Internal Review community with a wealth of valuable information they will use in the years to come."*

Mr. Minkow had given numerous well-received presentations at various law firms, *including the O'Melveny & Myers law firm, Mr. Petrocelli's firm.* Here is a quotation from a commendation letter received by Mr. Minkow from O'Melveny & Myers:

> *". . . Mr. Minkow also spoke recently to a group of over 30 associates and summer interns at my law firm on the psychology of fraud and related issues."*

Even Mr. Petrocelli's firm, O'Melveny & Myers, had used Mr. Minkow's services. Many prominent local community members spoke highly of FDI and its founder, and his background was certainly no secret.

So if the Fraud Discovery Institute was good enough for the SEC, the FBI, the IRS, the U.S. Army, the O'Melveny & Myers law firm, colleges and universities across the country, why wouldn't I consider using their services to locate the all-important whistleblower?

The Fraud Discovery Institute was a good potential candidate to locate the writer of the whistleblower letter for us, because it was without question that FDI had established strong relationships with the exact agencies looking at Lennar and that the anonymous whistleblower highlighted several times in the letter:

> *"I have been instructed to move every-thing back on the balance sheet as quickly as possible to avoid further inquiries from the FBI or the SEC enforcement agency."*
>
> *"Right now Lennar has a(n) SEC inquiry, and all the SEC needs is a party to come forth to highlight Lennar's improprieties."*

I had mentioned Mr. Minkow to a banker friend the day I had read the *Wall Street Journal* article on FDI, and to my surprise, the banker said that Mr. Minkow was a client of the bank and that he knew him well. The bank's chairman had personally recommended Mr. Minkow to the bank's chief credit officer, and the bank had opened accounts and had underwritten and made loans to Mr. Minkow and his church.

I read further regarding Mr. Minkow's fraud discovery operation, and found that he was held in high regard by the toughest and smartest of our country's regulatory and law enforcement agencies. I wanted access to those agencies because otherwise Lennar would just overwhelm and bury me, keep my money, and move on to the next victim. That chance conversation led to a meeting with Mr. Minkow toward the end of November of 2008.

Soon I received a proposal from FDI. The Fraud Discovery Institute's concept was to use a website outlining various abuses that Lennar was engaged in regarding partners, lenders, and employees and inviting commentary and discreet feedback from others, hopefully including the writer of the whistleblower letter.

FDI BEGAN WORKING on a report outlining specific abuses and fraudulent conduct by Lennar, and shared drafts from time to time. However, on January 9, 2009 Minkow and FDI decided on their own to electronically publish a document they had created, had submitted to me for preliminary review, and that they termed a Red Flags Report. I had not authorized publication of this report, but the contents of it were not only generally accurate, they were in some cases even prescient. The general contents of the report have been more than validated over time. And that was Stuart Miller's real problem.

CHAPTER TWELVE

The Red Flags Report

WHAT WAS IT about publication of the Red Flags Report on January 9, 2009 that was sufficient to get Stuart Miller out of bed and dispatch him to a remote CNBC studio for an impromptu interview?

Just the day before, on January 8, 2009, J.P. Morgan (ever heard of them?) had published a report questioning Lennar's market valuation and calling for a significantly lower price target for the stock. Among the factors cited by the Morgan report were: "larger than expected impairment charges; weaker than expected order growth; and unexpected challenges in its joint venture arrangements."

In plain English, the Morgan report was saying that its expectations were that Lennar would continue to lose money, keep shrinking, and nobody outside the company really knew what the real exposure was in the opaque and mysterious off-balance-sheet joint ventures. The new Lennar share price target identified by Morgan was $8.50 per share.

Where was the fire-department-class response to the J.P. Morgan report? If maintaining the stock price was so important, and a 3 or 4 point decline would be so catastrophic, why didn't Miller suit up, slide down the pole, and go put the J.P. Morgan fire out the day before? Actually, it doesn't appear that Lennar ever responded to the J.P. Morgan report, even though if the report was well read and well received, the Lennar stock price would start repricing downward in a New York minute.

The claims cooked up and filed by Miller and Petrocelli in connection with publication of the Red Flags Report included "market manipulation" of Lennar stock, even though there wasn't a single mention of Lennar stock in the FDI report. But the J.P. Morgan report specifically recommended a lower stock price for Lennar. Just who was manipulating the stock price?

After all, the claims that have emanated from Lennar over the publication of the allegedly *"false and scurrilous"* Red Flags Report center on damages purportedly suffered by Lennar as a result of a temporary decline in the price of its stock. Here J.P. Morgan was specifically calling for and indeed advocating a downward adjustment in the stock price!

But Lennar is much smaller than J.P. Morgan, does business with other divisions of J.P. Morgan, and Lennar would have no chance of intimidating and overwhelming them even if they didn't like the conclusions reached in their report. But maybe FDI could be intimidated and overwhelmed.

So, Lennar sued FDI, my company and me over a temporary decline in the Lennar Corp stock price allegedly caused by the publication of the Red Flags Report. And for a variety of reasons the stock did decline a few points for a few months, but the decline was from a January 9, 2009 price of $11.42 a share to an average price of $8.47. Was it the J.P. Morgan report, which called for a price of $8.50, was it the Red Flags Report, or a combination of both, or neither?

And guess what: less than six weeks earlier, that's right — less than six weeks — the Lennar stock price had declined to a low of $3.64. The brief decline attributed by them to the FDI report was from a price of $11.42 to an average of about $8.50 a share. Who did they sue for the $3.64 share price? The New York Stock Exchange? Or those damned investors who didn't see or appreciate what a valuable enterprise this company was just a few weeks earlier? The fact is that it is a volatile stock in a volatile business in a volatile market.

Lennar didn't sue J.P. Morgan, but Lennar's response to the Red Flags Report has been beyond belief. In addition to a blanket denouncement of the report, describing it as *"false and scurrilous"*, and denying the validity of each and every Red Flag in the report, they have spent tens and tens of millions of dollars of Lennar shareholder money engaging in coast-to-coast retaliatory litigation and media onslaught on the advice of Petrocelli and with the enthusiastic support of Miller.

Lennar and its lawyers launched kill-the-messenger lawsuits asserting new claims totaling hundreds of millions of dollars, engaged in a national smear campaign, and made oral and written false statements to the U.S. Attor-

ney's office in Miami, Florida. Those false statements ultimately resulted in an unwarranted prison sentence for
FDI's Mr. Minkow after Lennar exhausted his resources
and he was unable to properly defend against Lennar's concocted claims.

Lennar and its lawyers made false statements in the California courts, rigged and gamed the court system in
Miami, co-opted one or more judges, and have undermined
and compromised the legal system coast to coast in an all-
out effort to draw attention away from their fraudulent and
criminal acts. These actions were designed by Lennar to
discredit the FDI report, the author, my company, and me,
and to conceal the author of the whistleblower letter
(which of itself may just be a Sarbanes Oxley violation).

Lennar's and Miller's problem was that not only was
the Red Flags Report generally accurate, and in no way
"false and scurrilous", but so was the anonymous whistleblower letter. And together they opened the door to criminal prosecution of Lennar and certain of its executives if
the message and the messengers weren't silenced and destroyed immediately.

As stated above, the Red Flags Report was generally accurate and in fact actually quite prescient in some areas.
Let's take a point by point look at the Red Flags in the report and also incorporate the many facts, events, documents, and even testimony from key Lennar executives that
have come to light after publication of the report that clar-
ify, validate, and even strengthen the basic premises outlined in the report.

Red Flags #1 & 2. — Offshore Accounts and Money Laundering.

Red Flags 1 and 2 deal with a curious financial transaction that took place in late September 2007 involving Jon Jaffe and Jaffe's purported mortgage lender — a Mr. Robert Venneri and his two lending companies Gulfstream Finance Inc. and Canyon Finance Inc., and lastly a Mr. Bruce Elieff.

FDI had picked up the scent of a questionable transaction in these two Red Flags. FDI identified the key players correctly, but like many fraud investigations, it took more digging, hitting a few dead ends, and the passage of time before a fortuitous lawsuit filed in Orange County, California helped immensely to figure what was most likely going on with Jaffe and his "lender."

Jaffe and his family own and occupy an ostentatious home at 88 Emerald Bay in Laguna Beach. According to property reports, by the first of September 2007, this home had been mortgaged with both first and second Wells Fargo Bank secured loans in an aggregate amount of $5,000,000. On September 27, 2007 a new third mortgage appeared for an additional $5,000,000 — doubling the debt load to an aggregate of $10,000,000!

It is important to note at this juncture that by 2007 the credit markets, real estate markets, and the U.S. economy were going off of a cliff. Especially in California. Mortgage markets seized up, and real estate credit had all but dried up even for the most credit-worthy borrowers.

As a consequence, high-end residential real estate prices

in California began a steep decline that didn't level off until 2011. Lenders were failing in record numbers. Borrowers couldn't pay. Loans were unavailable in part because in many cases the prospective collateral was declining in value at a rate of 1% or more per month. Impossible to underwrite a loan under those conditions.

And loan demand fell precipitously as well since the economic storm was increasing in intensity day by day, the economic outlook was murky, and prudent borrowers stayed on the sidelines to wait out the storm.

Lennar reported its largest loss in the history of the company that year. Homes weren't selling. Foreclosures were skyrocketing. No sensible borrower, especially the COO of a housing company, would double down on debt under those conditions. In fact Lennar itself was in trouble and desperately trying to shed debt as quickly as possible.

Even the least risky 1st trust deed-secured mortgages were almost impossible to obtain, and 2nd trust deed secured loans were a thing of the past. The next loan category in the secured-loan pecking order, 3rd trust deed loans, were available only under special conditions and were invariably very, very, expensive, and hard to get. Those types of loans were also underwritten carefully and extensively, and they were carefully documented.

It was the golden rule: 3rd trust deed lenders had the gold, and they made the rules. And 3rd trust deed lenders are a different breed in the mortgage lending world. They operate just barely over the balance point between fear and greed. There is no secondary market for 3rd trust deed secured mortgages, so 3rd trust deed lenders, unlike primary mortgage lenders, make loans as if it is their own money. That is because it most often is their own money.

Loaning in a junior secured position into a market where collateral was declining at 1% per month was not for the faint hearted, because 3rd trust deed lenders not only had to be willing to take the risk of default by the borrower, but also had to be prepared to pay off or keep current the senior mortgages on the collateral, or they risked getting foreclosed out and losing their principal.

Thus it would be very rare even in normal markets to see a large 3rd trust deed loan behind equally large 1st and 2nd secured loans, and the risk pricing for such a loan would be excruciating.

And let's face it: any borrower willing to pay the exorbitant fees and interest rates that come with 3rd trust deed lending needs the money, so the credit risk is even more amplified if you are 3rd trust deed lender.

So, with the backdrop of economic conditions in 2007 (and 2007 looked like a picnic compared to 2008), let's look at Mr. Jaffe as a prospective borrower, the transaction in question, the collateral, the lender, and the purported terms of the loan transaction.

The financial transaction in question is a 3rd trust deed mortgage secured by Mr. Jaffe's principal residence and is in a junior position to two notes payable to Wells Fargo totaling around $5,000,000. The note date is February 4, 2008, is effective October 29, 2007, and purports to replace a $5,000,000 note dated September 27, 2007.

Looking at Jaffe as a prospective borrower would make any lender queasy in 2007, especially a sharp-eyed risk player like a 3rd trust deed lender. Not to mention in 2008.

Home builders like Lennar were in deep trouble. With Jaffe the Plow Horse as chief operating officer, Lennar reported the largest loss in the history of the company in 2007: over $1,900,000,000! Home sales absolutely depended on healthy and functional mortgage markets, and those markets were all but shut down. Lennar itself was a subprime lender, and the party was over for the subprime lenders, "liar loan" lenders, collateralized mortgage obligations, and other mortgage abuses that fueled the homebuilders in prior years and then brought the U.S. financial markets to the brink of disaster.

Lennar slashed salaries and suspended bonuses in an effort to stay afloat. Stock options held by the Lennar executives were so far underwater the executives, like Jaffe, needed snorkels and fins to just analyze how worthless their options were at that point. Mr. Jaffe's publically reported salary and benefits totaled a pre-tax $800,000. This is also known as $400,000 in California after state and federal tax.

$400,000 of after tax income would be inadequate to even pay the interest on his first, second, and prospective third mortgages on his home much less have money left over to pay bills and living expenses.

Various appraisals of Mr. Jaffe's home have been put forth in the context of evaluating the security available to secure three mortgages, but there is one fact no one has disputed: high — end homes in California began a steep descent in value in 2007 and everybody knew it. That type of value decline invariably feeds on itself and nobody could realistically evaluate when and at what level the market would stabilize.

And, speaking of appraisals, it is clear looking back that Jaffe is the master of inflated appraisals. He was the primary Lennar manager responsible for the LandSource LLC debacle that certainly involved inflated appraisals and fraudulent cash flow projections to obtain a $1,400,000,000 loan from a Barclays Bank syndicate in March of 2007. And, in November of 2006, according to a recent lawsuit filed by the FDIC, Lennar defrauded the FDIC specifically by using inflated appraisals and straw buyers. So an appraisal from Jaffe should be viewed with these facts in mind and an appropriate degree of skepticism.

An examination of the Jaffe 3rd trust deed mortgage note itself, the terms of the note, and the timing of the placement of the note reveal that it is unlikely that such a loan could have been obtained on an arm's length basis at that point in time. The market terms for such a loan — if you could get it — would be at least 10—12% annual interest, paid monthly, and a 10 point (10 percent) fee in front.

Can one even visualize a standard loan application process for such a loan? Collateral inadequate and declining in value? Check. No identifiable ability of borrower to service the loan or repay principal? Check. Hey, wait — that sounds a lot like LandSource!

The loan documents and specifically the note itself contain material errors, for example the wrong property address, and also contain terms no arms-length lender would ever agree to under any circumstances. For example, the note rate is 8%, well below market, with no fees payable, and here is the default clause in its entirety:

> *"Upon the occurrence and during the continuance of an Event of Default hereunder, the outstanding principal amount hereunder, shall bear interest at a rate per annum equal to the rate of five percent (5%) per annum."*

So, a sophisticated lender would loan money on an arm's length basis at about half of market rate, in a junior position, on a declining asset, while credit has all but dried up, the borrower's income is inadequate to cover the interest, and the lender also agreed that in the event of default the penalty is a 40% reduction in rate? Rather unlikely. It is pretty likely the Wells Fargo default clauses aren't quite so forgiving. In fact, they probably have the right to seize your children until you pay.

The purported lenders on Jaffe's 3rd trust deed secured loan were Gulfstream Finance Inc. and Canyon Finance Inc., two of Mr. Venneri's companies. The Fraud Discovery Institute noted in the Red Flags Report and subsequent reports that there was ample evidence that the $5,000,000 note was not likely to be an arm's length transaction and that Mr. Venneri may well be engaged in money-laundering activity with Mr. Jaffe.

It is not an uncommon practice to repatriate undeclared funds from offshore accounts via tax-free mortgages and other types of loans made by ostensible third parties. This practice is covered in detail in *The Wolf of Wall Street* by Jordan Belfort in an entertaining and informative chapter about the practical aspects of money laundering.

Lennar's January 12, 2009 press release in response to the Red Flags Report addressed some of the issues concerning the loan and stated in part that the funds for Jaffe's loan were indeed obtained from Mr. Venneri through his company, Canyon Finance Inc, and that Mr. Venneri also secured loans for Bruce Elieff, a SunCal employee.

The Lennar January 12, 2009 press release stated:

Jon was referred to Mr. Venneri by Jon's personal attorney . . .

Jaffe testified on August 13, 2012 that his attorney was Jim Weisz who at the time was with the firm of Rutan & Tucker. Mr. Weisz's practice was focused on wealth planning, including offering advice on asset protection and offshore trusts. And for an executive like Jaffe, engaged in nonstop fraudulent conduct, an asset protection plan would be foremost in his mind.

So who made the Jaffe loan, if there ever was a real loan in the first place? A lawsuit was filed in Orange County, California and the Cayman Islands on April 9, 2010 by Gray I CPB naming as defendants Mr. Elieff, his wife, and Gulfstream Finance Inc. (Venneri) asserting their participation a $140,000,000 money laundering scheme. Note that these are three of the four players in the FDI report. Analysis of this lawsuit and the money laundering allegations contained within shed light on this question. Additional actions were also filed at that time in the Cayman Islands by the plaintiff seeking more information on Mr. Venneri's activities there.

In the Orange County lawsuit:

> *"This action involves a fraudulent scheme created, masterminded, and designed by Bruce, Kathy, and Gulfstream possibly with the aid and assistance of others, to create fraudulent encumbrances on the Subject Properties, and possibly other assets, so there would be no equity in the Subject Properties and other assets to satisfy the indebtedness."*

> In the Cayman filing: *"This is an Application on behalf of the Plaintiff Gray I CPB, LLC ("Gray 1") for documentary and oral evidence from 16 intended witnesses to be produced pursuant to a Letter of Request issued to this court by the Superior Court of the State of California for the County of Orange (the "California court") and dated 9 January 2012."*

> *"In addition, I note that several of the intended witnesses are subject to the Money Laundering Regulations (as revised)."*

Sometime around 2001 Jon Jaffe confided to me personally that he maintained substantial offshore accounts, including life insurance wrap accounts that were used by him to trade securities among other things. He even stated that he could and did trade Lennar stock in those offshore accounts. And that other Lennar executives were participating as well.

It has been and continues to be my view that it is likely that the source of funds on the Venneri/Gulfstream/Canyon Finance loan is Mr. Jaffe himself, or a controlled offshore entity. Who else would offer those terms or be so careless with the loan security, repayment risks, default provisions, and documentation?

There are striking similarities between the $140,000,000 Eleiff loan and Mr. Jaffe's loan. Is it likely that Gulfstream Finance, Mr. Venneri's company, actually loaned $140,000,000 to Mr. Elieff in a junior position on a very small portfolio of residential properties in Orange County worth at the most a few million dollars? During the worst financial crisis since the Depression? If one had $140,000,000 at that point in time, perhaps the best place for it was under the mattress since banks were failing. But in any event, not junior under-secured real estate loans.

The explanation for Gulfstream's purported loan to Mr. Jaffe is more than likely that Mr. Venneri and Gulfstream were acting as a conduit to repatriate much-needed offshore dollars back to Mr. Jaffe. And that makes sense given Jaffe's after-tax salary versus his lavish lifestyle, and the fact that his bonuses had dried up and his stock options were worthless. Why would any sane residential borrower voluntarily double down in 2007 in the face of a serious economic collapse? Unless the default risk was exactly zero since it was Jaffe's money in the first place. Thus the ridiculous terms of the note and especially the default clause.

So, on balance, while FDI may not have had enough information initially to figure out exactly what was going on with Mr. Jaffe, Mr. Venneri, Gulfstream Finance Inc., Canyon Finance Inc., and Mr. Elieff, FDI certainly caught the scent of something most likely improper involving these people.

Based on the look-back and subsequent revelations, and who knows, there may be more coming, score Red Flags 1 and 2 for FDI. These two Red Flags are not *"false and scurrilous."* The score so far is FDI 2, Lennar 0.

Red Flag #3.—LandSource LLC.

The topic of LandSource LLC is covered in detail in Chapter 8, and it is a chilling story of fraud on a grand scale. In fact, it was maybe the largest single real estate fraud in California history. The Lennar executives cynically targeted pensioners, savers, lenders, suppliers, contractors, creditors, partners, and ultimately California tax payers. And Lennar and its sister company pocketed 1.4 billion dollars in the process. Not too shockingly, Jon Jaffe and Stuart Miller are the principal Lennar executives responsible for this outrageous fraud.

FDI was right on the money with this flag. There is nothing *"false and scurrilous"* about this Red Flag, so the score is FDI 3, Lennar 0.

Red Flag #4.—Inadequate Legal Disclosures by Lennar.

This flag deals with the fact that, before publication of the Red Flags report, Lennar included virtually no details or information in their public reporting on litigation facing the company, or indicated what legal exposure from various claims there may be to the company.

The FDI Report indicated that Lennar Corp's disclosures of pending litigation provided to the SEC were inadequate and constituted a material misrepresentation of the company's true financial condition by not properly disclosing potential exposure of filed lawsuits.

A review of Lennar SEC quarterly and annual reporting indicates that Lennar routinely had made essentially no disclosures of pending litigation prior to the Red Flags Report publication. There were many breach of contract, fraud, class action, and other lawsuits filed across the U.S. that were never reported in any SEC filing.

Our own research uncovered numerous lawsuits that certainly involved material claims and numbers that would warrant disclosure, but that information never made it into any 10Q or 10K. Also, the nature of the claims now differed materially from the garden-variety home defect claims that were the bulk of litigation concerning Lennar before Stuart Miller was put in charge of the company.

Now, the prevalent claims were based on claims like fraud, fraud in the inducement, and breach of contract. The cultural underpinnings of the company had changed dramatically with Stuart Miller and Jaffe running their shell

game with partners, lenders, and investors. This type of conduct was now a pattern and practice of Lennar—the Lennar
Way. And they got sued regularly for it.

After publication of the Red Flags Report, Lennar
changed its litigation reporting practices in direct response to
the report. Let Stuart Miller's own testimony in a deposition
taken in Miami on May 23, 2012 address this Red Flag issue:

*Q. So is it a fair summary of that response to say that, whereas
before these statements (the Red Flags Report) were made, Lennar would
disclose what it viewed as lawsuits that could have a material financial
impact on the company, whereas afterwards, in whatever particular for-
mat you chose, you were disclosing all lawsuits that the company was involved in?*

*A. "Disclosing all lawsuits" would be too aggressive, because as I
said, we weren't disclosing them individually, but we were disclosing
more information about the body of lawsuits that we had in our legal
backlog.*

*Q. But that distinction was correct before, if it was material enough
to have — a dollar-wise materially enough impact on the company, it
was disclosed?*

A. Right.

*Q. And nothing else was, and then afterwards, speaking categori-
cally, everything was disclosed?*

*A. I believe that to be a correct statement. We could go back and
look at the disclosures and find that I am wrong, but I believe that is
the case.*

Miller admitted that Lennar changed its litigation reporting policy after the publication of the Red Flags Report. And

they were now providing much more information to the public. How can this beneficial result be bad for the investing public? And how could this Red Flag # 4 be deemed *"false and scurrilous"* by anyone given the admissions that came right from Stuart Miller while testifying under oath. This proves the validity of this flag beyond a shadow of doubt. This one isn't even a close call.

There is nothing *"false or scurrilous"* about this Red Flag, so the score is now FDI 4, Lennar 0.

Red Flag #5 — Lennar Shell Game.

This Red Flag alleged that Lennar manipulated the numbers and shifted money between ventures as needed. We need to look no further than the admissions by Mike White, the west coast Lennar CFO, about *"improper"* and *"wrong"* payments to LandSource from our Bridges development company on this one. His testimony is covered in Chapter 8 on LandSource. But we will look further.

Not only had Lennar hijacked our development company's funds to prop up LandSource, Lennar also drained other similarly situated ventures for the same purpose. In the hard-fought litigation discovery process we unearthed internal memos between Lennar accounting people that detailed the large sums drained from Lennar-managed but not wholly-owned enterprises to pay interest on a loan these entities didn't take out, for money they didn't get or use.

In an internal memo dated April 3, 2007 (written one month after the special dividend) a Lennar controller began the memo with the capitalized word OUCH!!! And for good reason. The memo was an interest bill for the month of March 2007 to the numerous ventures under Lennar control, and recites:

"As you can see, the amounts have increased significantly from prior months. This is due to the size of LandSource's new debt facility . . . "

Why would our company or any other Lennar-managed company be paying interest on a fraudulently-arranged loan to pay a special dividend to only Lennar and its sister company?

And it got worse. Further discovery revealed that Lennar dropped the pretense of "cash management" and simply began wiring our development company's income directly to LandSource. Bridges membership deposits were deposited directly into LandSource's bank account.

The whistleblower letter detailed *"As I review each joint venture, I am finding countless abuse(s) and improper accounting treatment."*

Remember Marc Chasman? One of his specialties within the company was to run a scam where Lennar shifted most of their overhead, including employee costs, to joint ventures. This made their wholly owned developments considerably more profitable, but at the expense of managed ventures. Chasman testified on this matter and looked like a bunny in the headlights.

And then there were the Lennar pigs-at-the-trough slurping up any available cash from our Bridges development company on a regular basis as outlined elsewhere in this book.

There is nothing *"false or scurrilous"* about this Red Flag. We were uniquely and unfortunately positioned to observe and feel the detrimental effects of this shell game run by Lennar. Score this one for FDI, and score is now FDI 5, Lennar 0.

Red Flag # 6—Off-Balance Sheet Joint Ventures

The whistleblower letter stated that:

"I have been involved in unwinding all of material Lennar off-balance sheet joint ventures." I have been instructed to move everything back on to the balance sheet as quickly as possible to avoid further inquiries from either the FBI or the SEC Enforcement Agency."

Stuart Miller testified extensively on this topic in deposition and although it is difficult to extract cogent, illuminating, and on-point testimony from his non-stop alternate-universe diatribe, nonetheless he did provide some direct insight into Lennar's decision-making process to unwind the myriad of Lennar off-balance sheet joint ventures.

Guess what: after analysis of Miller's sworn testimony and the responses he gave in his appearance on CNBC the day of FDI's publication, Miller's testimony and responses on CNBC support FDI's Red Flag #6 one hundred percent.

And this is hugely important, because Stuart Miller had been lying under oath, lying to U.S. Attorneys, lying to the media, and lying to Lennar's stockholders while squandering their money on gigantic legal bills and costs to perpetuate the lies.

Lennar assailed FDI for highlighting the fact that Lennar held huge and opaque off-balance sheet positions in literally hundreds of real estate joint ventures around the country. "False and Scurrilous," they shouted!

And with a steep decline in real estate activity and a decline in values well under way by the FDI publication date, FDI wasn't the only one out there that openly questioned the potential exposure to Lennar, and thus its shareholders and lenders, to literally hundreds of non-disclosed ventures involving billions in off-balance sheet debt.

Miller tried to make it sound like the off-balance sheet positions held by Lennar were in a healthy and sound condition as of the date of the FDI publication. And that the FDI report triggered an unwarranted and costly unwinding process after publication of the report in January 2009.

Nothing is further from the truth, and you don't have to go beyond Miller's own testimony to prove it. In his CNBC appearance, also on January 9, 2009, the very date of publication of the FDI report, here is what he said:

This excerpt is taken from the live televised interview with Diane Olick of CNBC:

Q. Given that, though, Mr. Miller, as soon as this news hit this morning, many analysts on Wall Street said they have always been skeptical of Lennar's disclosures, they didn't want to give credence to what this report was saying, we always take everything with a grain of salt. Why is the street so skeptical citing lack of transparency in your disclosures to the SEC?

A. Well there is no question throughout the past years, because we have done so many ventures and each one is so unique it is difficult to give the street the kind of transparency they would like to have if they were able to look at each one individually.

Q. One analyst said he had to "black box" Lennar saying you really could not tell anything?

A. Well, I am not sure what "black box" means, we have a pretty good relationship with all of the analysts on the street and we have kept an open door with our investors, and we tried to give them as much disclosure as possible, but at our peak, we had over 300 ventures, and are now down over 60 percent, but the amount of disclosure that would have been required to sate the appetite of the many people that were asking was too extensive or too voluminous.

Q. Do you feel at this point that divesting or spinning off the joint ventures is because of the disclosure issue or the downturn in the market?

A. Well, I think that it's primarily about the downturn in the market. Many of the ventures started out to be optomistic about land that was involved, and that land has been severely impaired, and we have taken those impairments.

Diane Olick — Mr. Miller, thank you so much for being on the program.

And we thank you for coming on the program too, Mr. Miller. The last question and answer puts the lie to the notion that the FDI report harmed Lennar by highlighting Lennar's off-balance sheet joint ventures and caused Lennar to unwind its positions. Let's just savor Miller's on-the-air national appearance on CNBC and repeat exactly what he just said:

Q. Do you feel at this point that divesting or spinning off the joint ventures is because of the disclosure issue or the downturn in the market?

A. — Well, I think that it's primarily about the downturn in the market. Many of the ventures started out to be optomistic about land that was involved, and that land has been severely impaired, and we have taken those impairments.

This puts the lie to Miller's sworn testimony taken in depositions in regard to why and when Lennar began to unwind their mammoth off-balance sheet joint venture positions. It puts the lie to representations made by Miller and his attorneys to the Miami U.S. Attorney's office about the effects of the *"false and scurrilous"* Red Flags Report, and it puts the lie to the lawsuit brought by Lennar in Miami claiming damages for publication of the Red Flags Report. And it is a crime to lie to a prosecutor or a U.S. Attorney. It should be a crime to file false and frivolous lawsuits.

Miller appeared on CNBC just a few hours after the FDI publication. A few hours. Yet he blamed FDI for publishing *"false and scurrilous"* information regarding Lennar's off-balance sheet joint ventures and causing Lennar to have to unwind their positions to provide more transparency to the street and the enforcement agencies. What did he do, unwind them on the way to the CNBC studio that day?

It gets better: here is a quote from the J.P Morgan report published the day before the FDI Red Flags Report:

"While JV risk should remain an overhang . . . exposure has continued to be reduced. Specifically, LEN has continued to reduce its JV exposure over the last several quarters."

In Lennar's press release of January 12, 2009 they stated

on the subject of off-balance sheet Joint Ventures:

"Lennar has included extensive financial disclosure regarding its JVs on its quarterly conference calls with analysts and investors and its SEC filings."

Oh really? Then why did many analysts view Lennar as a "black box", and recommended avoiding the stock due to lack of disclosure? And how many "quarters" had passed between the January 9, 2009 publication date and the January 12, 2009 press release three days later?

It is telling that the market got a chance to listen to Miller's explanation of their position on the JV issue and other issues and still continued to sell stock. If it was a credibility contest, Miller lost. And he had his chance. It was like open-mic Friday on CNBC and he had the opportunity to say anything he wanted.

The reality was that the Street was quite aware and concerned about Lennar's off-balance sheet joint venture problems long before the January 9, 2009 Red Flags publication date. That was crystal clear in the CNBC interview, and the J.P. Morgan report. And the unwind process started well before the FDI report.

Miller's testimony given under oath in his deposition is all the more remarkable since the testimony was given in conjunction with the gigantic claims filed by Lennar over the *"false and scurrilous"* nature of FDI's publication.

Miller, in page after page of deposition testimony, was desperately trying to stick to the little story rehearsed with his lawyers about FDI's report being the primary cause of

Lennar having to begin the JV unwind process. Not pressure from the Street. Not economics. Not an imploding real estate economy. Not plummeting land prices. Just FDI. And the more he testified, the more ridiculous and comical the effort became.

Let's look at Miller's testimony. On May 23, 2012 he testified as follows:

Q. "Did the company (Lennar) make a strategic decision to start unwinding joint ventures following January 2009?" (The FDI publication)

A. "... There is no question that after January 2009—we certainly pushed to address that part of the business, the joint venture component of the business."

But then, when pressed on the issue:

Miller — "We had about 300 partnerships at our peak, let's say, and today we're probably — we probably have 30."

Q. And why was there so much unwinding of partnerships from the peak at 300 down to the current level at 30?

A. Well, in some instances, it — in some instances it had to do with — in some instances it had to do with the fact that the market was deteriorating and the reason for the partnership had ceased to — ceased to exist, the development had stopped or stalled, equity positions, in some instances, had been wiped out."

And when Miller told Diane Olick on January 9, 2009:

"... I think it is primarily about the downturn in the market ...

and that land has been severely impaired, and we have taken those impairments."

"*Taken those Impairments*" is B School-speak for "we lost our ass", and that is exactly what the Street wanted to know: How much? What's next?

And Miller further testified under oath on May 23, 2012:

Q. I think you indicated earlier the consequences to the January 9th statements, and subsequent statements, was that Lennar became more — disclosed more to the market about its businesses than it had before. Can you elaborate on that for me? What additional things did you start to disclose that you had, up until that point, not disclosed?

A. Oh boy. You know, as it related to joint ventures, we started to specifically delineate; but I'd have to go back and look at some of this, but I think we started to actually give selected financial data relative to our largest joint ventures, we endeavored to give a lot more information about specific joint ventures, again, to assuage a queasy market's concerns about what these — what entities might be."

Queasy Market? Not FDI? Miller then goes on for a little bit about Enron, and, as usual, Miller bristled at any mention of Enron in Red Flag #6, but note that he hired the lawyer defending the CEO of Enron. Who actually did go to jail for a very long time. Talk about tempting the fates!

And speaking of Enron, Miller testified:

"Again, the misinformation that was put out there (The FDI Report) was to

> *draw a direct parallel between our joint*
> *ventures and those of Enron.*
>
> *And I don't know if you followed*
> *the Enron program, but as the market*
> *understands Enron, there were a lot of*
> *joint ventures where there were no assets*
> *to support the venture . . . and as they*
> *collapsed and evaporated there was noth-*
> *ing there."*

Interesting comment by Miller since he also testified on the very same day on the implosion of various Lennar joint ventures:

> *Well, in some instances, it — in*
> *some instances it had to do with — in*
> *some instances it had to do with the fact*
> *that the market was deteriorating and*
> *the reason for the partnership had*
> *ceased to exist, the development had*
> *stopped or stalled, equity positions, in*
> *some instances, had been wiped out."*

Is there any material difference between *"as they collapsed and evaporated there was nothing there"*, and *"equity positions, in some instances, had been wiped out?"*

None, as far we can tell.

By Miller's own admission the FDI Report forced Lennar to provide more transparency, and how could that hurt? The Street was openly skeptical in the first place about Lennar's real exposure, with some analysts dubbing Lennar a "Black Box", and avoiding the stock.

And FDI's report on this Red Flag included quotes from other published blogs highly critical of Lennar's mystery off-balance sheet JV positions. Where was Lennar's thunderous and litigious response to those already-published and highly critical blogs?

Any notion that Lennar unwound billions of dollars in off-balance sheet exposure because of a *"false and scurrilous"* report by FDI is ludicrous. In over ten pages of a deposition of Miller on the matter, his story and their fabricated claims fall apart completely. They were already unwinding their positions by the date of the report, and simply continued the process.

And some of the positions were *"unwinding"* themselves according to Miller. And the definition of *"unwinding"* in that context is also called *"imploding" "losing" and "failing."*

And if the huge off-balance sheet JV business Lennar was involved in was healthy and profitable, does anybody really believe that, based on exactly one report, they would begin immediately shutting down the business, and scurry around like insects disposing of or shifting the assets in the words of the whistleblower *"as quickly as possible?"*

There is nothing *"false or scurrilous"* about this Red Flag. Score this one for and now the score is now FDI 6, Lennar 0.

Red Flag # 7—Lennar's Chinese Drywall Exposure.

The Fraud Discovery Institute Red Flags Report spotlighted

Lennar's exposure to Chinese drywall installed in many Lennar-built homes. Lennar had built hundreds if not thousands of homes containing cheap imported Chinese drywall. This drywall was highly defective and toxic. It made the homes essentially unlivable, and the remedy was to virtually tear down the home and start over. Which was very costly and was entirely attributable to the builder, Lennar.

There was very little reporting by Lennar on this issue until the Red Flags Report was published. Lennar responded to the report in the January 12, 2009 press release and certainly didn't deny the problem. But they still concealed the magnitude of the problem.

Within two months of publication of the Red Flags Report Lennar filed multi-million dollar suits against Chinese drywall suppliers, began taking significant reserves against Chinese drywall exposure, and was forced to rebuild many homes that contained the noxious drywall.

On March 30, 2009, less than three months after publication of the FDI report, a *South Florida Business Journal* headline read:

Chinese Drywall Class Action Lawsuit Targets Lennar Corp.

The story goes on to report that "Miami-based Lennar Corp. has been targeted with a class action lawsuit in the growing product liability issue over Chinese drywall."

And Lennar's 10Q for the period ending in May 31, 2009 contained the following disclosure:

Item 1. Legal Proceedings.—
As of July 10, 2009 the Company is aware of 41 Florida state court lawsuits and two federal class action suits that have been filed against the Company by homeowners and their family members in connection with defective Chinese drywall. There are other related state and federal cases in which the Company is not a party. All federal cases have been consolidated for discovery and pre-trial purposes in the Eastern District of Louisiana pursuant to the multi-district litigation ("MDL") procedure. The Company has sued in Miami-Dade circuit court the entire supply chain, including the Chinese and German manufacturers of the defective drywall. Lennar has move to abate all 41 state court actions pursuant to Florida's law allowing builders to repair. Lennar is attempting to perfect service of its complaint on the Chinese defendants.

Any way you slice it, this was a big problem for the company and should have been disclosed earlier and in more detail. The FDI Red Flags Report caused much more public disclosure of this problem than otherwise would have been available. How could that be bad for investors?

The Chinese drywall Red Flag was not in any way *"false and scurrilous."* On the contrary, the report was generally accurate on this topic, and ahead of Lennar's public reporting on the true magnitude of this issue.

Again, this flag isn't even a close call. There was nothing *"false or scurrilous"* about this Red Flag regarding Lennar's exposure to problems related to Chinese drywall. Many media outlets reported on this issue, and their reporting wasn't materially different than the FDI report.

There is nothing *"false or scurrilous"* about this Red Flag. Score this one for FDI, and the score is now FDI 7, Lennar 0.

Red Flag # 8 — FDI's Use of the Term: "Ponzi Scheme."

Much has been made about use of the term "Ponzi" in the FDI report regarding Lennar, and whether or not this term was applicable to Lennar's business conduct. A good starting point to analyze and try to answer this question would be to first seek an acceptable definition of the term Ponzi scheme in today's world.

Fortunately, we don't have to go very far to find a workable definition. Here is one right from a leading Lennar Board member, Irving Bolotin.

On February 17, 2010 Mr. Bolotin testified in a deposition under oath as to his state of mind regarding the definition of a Ponzi scheme:

Q. "In your mind, what does it mean that a ccorporation is run like a Ponzi scheme? What does that mean to you?"

A. "You take money from one venture and then you put it —
you pay off people who are expecting returns in one venture from money
that you receive from people who are investing in another venture."
   Q. "Robbing Peter to pay Paul?"
   A. "Robbing Bernie to pay his stockholders."

And an even more clear definition of the term Ponzi scheme was given under oath by Lennar's Chief Financial Officer Bruce Gross on December 2, 2013:

   Q. Can you explain to the jury what a Ponzi scheme is?
   A. A Ponzi scheme is a fraudulent operation whereby money is
stolen from investors — that's the simple way to explain it.

That is certainly "the simple way" to explain my experience with Lennar. And the experience of many, many others. Thank you director Mr. Bolotin, and thank you, CFO Gross.

The use of the term Ponzi scheme has certainly evolved since Charles Ponzi's eponymous scheme in the 1920's. The modern day use of the term has come to mean a description of a wide range of fraudulent conduct.

Cases in point: there are numerous recent articles in the *Wall Street Journal* and other national publications quoting some of the most sophisticated and influential people in the financial, political, and journalism world using the term Ponzi scheme. All of these people quoted in the articles must, of necessity, measure and use their words carefully. For example, Bill Gross formerly of giant bond fund Pimco can move markets and he has been widely quoted describing the equity markets as a Ponzi scheme. William Ackman of Pershing Square has described the Herbalife Company as a Ponzi scheme. A Forbes article refers to the Social Security System as a Ponzi Scheme. No litigation ensued as a result of these comments.

But let's just stay with Lennar director Mr. Bolotin and CFO Gross's definitions given under oath. Mr. Bolotin's definition of a Ponzi scheme fits the LandSource swindle perfectly:

"You take money from one venture" . . . (the Bridges development company) . . . *"and transfer it to another venture"* . . . (LandSource).

Thereby *"robbing Bernie to pay his stockholders."*

Well, at least one stockholder benefitted for sure from the LandSource swindle: Mr. Miller and his family were both the controlling shareholders in Lennar and interest holders in LNR. And both of these entities benefitted immensely from the 1.4 billion dollar special dividend paid out of LandSource. But the special dividend payment was much to the detriment of CALPERS pension holders, investors in Barclays loan syndicate, the unsecured creditors of the failed LandSource company, and many others, including me.

A reasonable definition of a Ponzi scheme appears to be any scheme that is designed to fraudulently obtain money from investors and/or lenders through a non-economically viable entity by masking the true financial condition of the entity and then transferring out or removing the fraudulently obtained funds.

Does LandSource come to mind? The LandSource unsecured creditors lawsuit stated:

"LandSource painted a fraudulent picture of its corporate health."

And there is nothing to say that a Ponzi scheme can't be uncovered beneath a seemingly legitimate business. Bernie Madoff operated a well-respected market making and stock trading firm in addition to his now more well-known activities. Enron had legitimate businesses in addition to their empty-shell off balance sheet ventures (sound familiar?). WorldCom had plenty of legitimate businesses but the company was rife with accounting fraud.

Lennar is now a predatory company, but is still dressed up in drag as a homebuilder. Certainly a portion of their activities fits the definition of a Ponzi scheme as articulated by their own director, their own CFO, and the unsecured creditors lawsuit.

So there was no wonder Miller went wild over the use of the term Ponzi scheme, and the comparisons to Enron. The truth hurt, and he knew exactly where Petrocelli's other high-profile client was currently living.

There is nothing *"false or scurrilous"* about this Red Flag. Score this one for FDI, and the score is now FDI 8, Lennar 0.

Red Flag # 9—Lennar's RICO conduct.

This Red Flag deals with the fact that Lennar's conduct fits the definition of racketeering and therefore exposes the company and certain of its officers to RICO statutes. And treble damages.

Congress passed the RICO act as part of the Organized Crime Control Act of 1970. RICO stands for Racketeer Influenced and Corruption Organizations Act. The specific goal of RICO is to punish the use of an enterprise to engage in certain criminal activities.

All that is required under the Act are at least two acts of racketeering activity within a ten year period to risk exposure to these statutes. FDI's conclusion was that Lennar Corporation, its senior management, and its subsidiaries had engaged in apparent fraudulent behavior over a sustained period of time that appeared to easily meet and exceed the civil RICO burden.

It is not necessary to go into a lengthy analysis here to support that contention because there is an entire chapter of this book devoted to this subject. The analysis in Chapter 19 supports this contention in every way, and the argument is compelling. This Red Flag as anything but *"false"* or *"scurrilous."*

Score this one for FDI, and the score is now FDI 9, Lennar 0.

Red Flag #10—Summary of the FDI Red Flags.

It is fair to say that upon close analysis the Red Flags Report, while not perfect, is anything but *"false and scurrilous."* A reasoned and well-researched look-back proves there is a factual basis for all of the main themes in the report.

Lennar and its lawyers' efforts to deny the validity of the

report, to suppress on-going publication of the report, and to silence and punish those involved have been extraordinary. But simply screaming *Liar! False and Scurrilous!* Is no match for a careful and reasoned analysis. The report was and is valid in all major respects.

I have a firm belief that the truth will come out. There isn't a fact in this book that can't be backed up by a document or a transcript of testimony from the Lennar executives. So far, you will note that almost all of the support for the validity of the Red Flags comes right from the mouths of the Lennar executives, Lennar's Board members, the invaluable information available from the look-back process, and analysis of events that took place subsequent to the publishing of the report.

And looking at how far Lennar has taken the pushback on this report only confirms the validity of the contents, and just how close to the mark this report must have hit Lennar and its executives.

Question: why has Lennar, at the direction of Stuart Miller, spent over $100,000,000 on lawyers, legal costs, and executive resources, lied to U.S. Attorneys in Miami, abused, co-opted, and defrauded the court systems coast to coast?

Answer: Lennar's disproportionate response to the report can only be explained by one word: fear. Because the report correctly identifies Lennar as a crime in progress, and it is most certainly that.

In summary, there was no valid basis for Lennar and its lawyers to claim that the Red Flags Report was, in their own words, *"false and scurrilous."* It is overwhelmingly clear that it was anything but that.

CHAPTER THIRTEEN

Kill the Messengers

LENNAR FILED A lawsuit in Miami over a four page letter I sent on July 11, 2008 to the Lennar Board of Directors. The letter expressed my concern over the governance of Lennar, management of our jointly owned development, and the fact that they had misappropriated substantial funds, including my $37,500,000 capital contribution. I, of course, asked the Board to look into the situation and to expedite return of my money.

Lennar invited the letter. In case there is any dispute over whether or not a formal and Lennar-instituted mechanism for communication with the Board was in place at the time I wrote the letter to them, here is a verbatim quote from the January 12, 2009 press release put out by Lennar in response to the Red Flags Report:

> *"Lennar has created two mechanisms*
> *for the public, investors, associates and*
> *other interested parties to communicate*

their concerns directly to the company's Board of Directors. First, Lennar has retained an independent firm, The Network, to receive complaints anonymously and report those complaints directly to the Audit Committee of the Board of Directors, in addition to management. The Audit Committee receives a report of the investigation of each communication submitted.

In addition, Lennar provides an email address which can be used to communicate directly with the independent members of the Board of Directors. Our lead director, who is also the chairperson of the Independent Directors Committee, receives all messages sent to this email address. Both of these reporting systems are described in our annual proxy statement, and are regularly communicated to our associates. These reporting systems have been in place for more than four years as required by law and by the rules of the New York Stock Exchange."

Lennar expressly and publicly invited those with concerns to communicate directly with the Board of Directors. And note the use of the term "concerns." They weren't fishing for compliments. I did have concerns, I did write such a letter, and upon receipt of the letter they immediately filed a lawsuit in response. There is nothing on their website that says, "Oh and by the way, if we don't happen to like your letter then we will sue you immediately."

The primary purpose of the meritless Florida lawsuit they filed was to accelerate their resource exhaustion tactics, and to open a new litigation front in their Miami backyard.

Lennar, not long after filing the first complaint, filed new claims over the Red Flags Report published on January 9, 2009. These new claims alleged that the contents of the report were *"false and scurrilous"* and that as a result of publication Lennar Corp "suffered over $500,000,000 in damages" as a direct result of "a decline in the value of Lennar Corp stock." The original lawsuit and its subsequent amendments were, of course, orchestrated by Petrocelli, approved by Miller, paid for by shareholders, and designed to overwhelm us in legal fees and costs.

The whistleblower letter I received was dated October 30, 2008, just a little over two months before the publication of the Red Flags Report by FDI. The Red Flags Report incorporated the observations made by the anonymous whistleblower.

With an inside whistleblower with highly damaging information and an outside whistleblower, FDI, to contend with, Miller went ballistic and immediately authorized Lennar's growing army of lawyers to take any and all actions to crush and silence these whistleblowers. Both whistleblowers were alleging criminal conduct by Lennar. So what did Miller and Petrocelli do?

In addition to filing more meritless claims, they cooked

up a story about the alleged damages and the *"false and scurrilous"* nature of the FDI report and secretly approached
the U.S. Attorney's office in Miami and claimed that FDI
conspired to publish false statements about Lennar Corp
and its executive officers.

Petrocelli wrote letters to the U.S. Attorney's office outlining Lennar's contentions. These letters included elaborate charts, graphs, and "analysis" of the damages allegedly
suffered by Lennar as a result of the decline in stock price
attributed to the *"false and scurrilous"* Red Flags Report.

Nothing was further from the truth. Petrocelli and
Miller lied to the U.S. Attorneys in Miami to further their
civil litigation strategies. A careful point-by-point analysis
of the Red Flags Report clearly refutes the notion that the
report was *"false and scurrilous."*

And, in any event, Lennar did not own its stock, the
shareholders did. Not one shareholder ever even wrote a
letter regarding the alleged stock decline, much less filed a
complaint.

The letters to the U.S. Attorneys' office, approved by
Miller, signed by Petrocelli, and which are in our posses-
sion, reveal a chilling and egregious pattern of deceit and
outright lies to not one but two U.S. Attorneys. The bogus
letters purported to tie the publication of the Red Flags
Report to a decline in Lennar stock that, in turn, caused direct damage to Lennar Corp. To the tune of a half a billion
dollars. This was nonsense.

In fact, Stuart Miller and Daniel Petrocelli conspired to
make false statements to not one but two U.S. Attorneys in
order to obtain an advantage in civil litigation.

First, the FDI report was accurate in most respects and subsequent events played out and validated all of the main premises of the report.

Second, and this is the most telling of the falsity of Lennar's position. Lennar has never reported a loss to shareholders or the SEC in regard to or in connection with the publication of the Red Flags Report. Not one dollar. Ever. Why is this significant?

Stuart Miller is Chief Executive Officer of Lennar Corp. He is required to sign Lennar's quarterly, annual, and special reports to the SEC under penalty of perjury. This is thanks in part to the Sarbanes Oxley Act (which ironically was enacted as a direct result of the actions of another one of Petrocelli's clients, Jeffrey Skilling). The Sarbanes Oxley Act mandates financial fines and jail time for a Chief Executive Officer who signs a knowingly false report to the SEC. And knowingly false includes omissions of material key information, as well.

So, Mr. Miller with Mr. Sustana, Lennar's in-house general counsel, at his side has signed years of quarterly and annual financial reports on behalf of Lennar Corp since publication of the Red Flags Report, and none of those quarterly and annual financial reports contain any mention of a loss suffered by Lennar Corp as a result of publication of the Red Flags Report. Not one.

In a deposition taken on August 7, 2012, Stuart Miller testified on the subject of damages and timely reporting to the SEC. And whether Lennar ever reported the alleged damages to the government in any SEC filing. He fenced with the examining lawyer for over 15 pages of dialogue while feigning ignorance about whether Lennar ever re-ported an alleged $500,000,000 in damages suffered in the first quarter of 2009.

Even with a copy of the 10Q from the first quarter of 2009 placed in front of him, he continued to evade one simple question: did you or did you not sign a report under penalty of perjury to the SEC that contained any mention of the purported damages?

Of course there was no mention of the fabricated dam-ages in the 1st Quarter 2009 10Q or any subsequent 10Q or 10K filing by Lennar. This is because the damage claim was false and never existed.

So Mr. Miller, with general counsel Mr. Sustana's assis-tance, reviewed and signed Lennar's financial reports under penalty of go-to-jail perjury that contained no mention whatsoever of the alleged damages. Then, astoundingly, Miller and Sustana, along with Petrocelli, strolled down to the U.S. Attorney's office in Miami and claimed that the publication of the Red Flags Report was the cause of over $500,000,000 in damages to Lennar Corp, and that those involved should be prosecuted immediately.

Even setting aside the fact the FDI report was generally accurate, the only conclusion one can reach is that either Mr. Miller was signing false financial statements as Chief Executive Officer of Lennar, or he was lying to the U.S. Attorneys. Neither is a good idea, but he is certainly guilty of one or the other. Either one makes Mr. Miller eligible for a jail cell.

Let's look at Mr. Miller's sworn testimony on these topics:

In a deposition taken May 24, 2012 Mr. Miller testified
that he personally attended meetings with the U.S. Attorneys at the Justice Department.

*Q. Did you personally participate in discussions with the Justice
Department?*

A. Yes.

Q. Okay. When did that occur?

A. I don't recall the dates.

Q. What year?

A. Let's say, probably 2011.

Q. Was that at in-person meetings or telephonically?

A. In-person meetings.

*Q. How many in-person meetings did you attend with anyone
from the Justice Department?*

A. I seem to recall two.

Q. OK.

A. Maybe three.

Q. All in 2011?

*Q. No, maybe 2010 as well. It feels to me, as I sit here, like it
was over a broader period of time.*

But in a deposition taken August 7, 2012, Mr. Miller
testified in regard to SEC reporting requirements:

*Q. And I certainly respect not only Lennar's success and your
responsibilities, however I'm troubled because are these documents,
meaning the 10Q, submitted under penalty of perjury to the government?*

A. Sure.

Q. And you are the one ultimately responsible who signs off on them —

A. Yes.

Q. — Correct? Although your expert now with hindsight has generated this voluminous report, are there any references to damages caused by Minkow or Marsch in any 10Q?

A. I don't recall.

Q. When you signed under penalties of perjury, the 10 Q specifically for the quarter ending February 2009, excuse me, or any subsequent quarters, do you recall disclosing the injuries that Minkow and Marsch (allegedly) caused you?

A. I — I — I - I don't recall. I don't recall them being ascertained at the time so I don't recall.

As the s-s-s-stuttering indicates, this was a profoundly dishonest statement by Mr. Miller. Just three days after publication of the Red Flags Report, Lennar was already tying the Red Flags publication to a quantifiable decline in stock price in their January 12, 2009 press release. And Petrocelli's duplicitous letters to the U.S. Attorneys contained very precise damage numbers.

There was a regularly scheduled Lennar board meeting just four days after the FDI Red Flags Report publication. In the nine page minutes of the meeting on January 13, 2009, there is exactly one mention of the Fraud Discovery Institute's report buried in a section titled "Committee Reports." Here is the verbatim transcript of that section:

"He (Mr. Lapidus) then described for the Board the planned review by outside counsel of the allegations made against the Company

by the Fraud Discovery Institute. Mr. Lapidus concluded by describing the advice received from outside counsel on the investigation."

Does this sound like a company that just lost over $500,000,000 only four days earlier? Of course not. And now we know the "planned review" by "outside counsel" was to be performed by none other than Petrocelli himself.

Years later, in 2012, as the Florida litigation wore on, Lennar concocted a new damage theory trying to use the purported stock decline as a proxy for damage directly to Lennar Corp. There is no accepted methodology to calculate damages in this way, yet they did this because it was increasingly obvious that they never owned the stock, nothing false was published, no damage occurred, and their original claim of over $500,000,000 in damages due directly to a decline in the stock value was false and unsupportable.

The problem with this newly-concocted approach was the same problem they always had with this made-up claim: that Lennar Corp never reported damages on their signed-under-penalty-of-perjury financial reports to the SEC under any theory. Ever.

Also, materiality is no defense to not mentioning a dollar of loss in any SEC report. The materiality of the fabricated damage claim is the exact basis of claims in the Florida lawsuit, communications with the U.S. Attorneys in Miami, and the numerous false press releases organized by Mr. Petrocelli and Lennar. Most of us view a claim of over $500,000,000 as material.

Thus, using very precisely calculated, albeit false, damage claims, Lennar gamed the U.S Attorneys and engineered a forced plea and a settlement by Mr. Minkow after exhausting his resources. And the size of the alleged damages had everything to do with the extorted plea. It is a fact that any plea obtained through duress is inherently unreliable. And this coerced plea without doubt was obtained under duress because of the malicious machinations undertaken by Miller and Petrocelli.

But it wasn't the U.S. Attorneys at fault. Not even close. The fault lies with the Lennar executives and Petrocelli. Much like judges in various courtroom venues from San Diego to Miami, they were unknowingly across the table from some of the most skillful liars in the country.

And, as you will see in Chapter 16, Petrocelli overtly and repeatedly lied on the record to jurors in Miami. And co-opted a judge to do the same. So, a lawyer who will actively participate in undermining the legal system in a Miami courtroom would think nothing of lying to a U.S. Attorney just ten minutes away in another building.

I have known and worked with law enforcement people periodically for over thirty years, and have great respect for those in that profession. Even the ones that gave me a few speeding tickets. I deserved them.

All of them that I have met have taken the jobs at least in part for the opportunity to make the world a better and safer place. None took the job for the money because it isn't enough for the stressful and high risk profession they have chosen. Certainly many in, for example, a District Attorney or U.S. Attorney job view the position as a stepping stone to a more lucrative career in the private sector, and what is wrong with that? Practical real-world experience counts for a lot in a career path.

One problem in this case lies both in the power aggregated by prosecutors in the criminal justice system and the willingness of Lennar and its lawyers to blatantly lie to the U.S. Attorneys in Miami to further their civil litigation goals. This proved to be a dangerous combination, which was the idea in the first place.

A book was published in 2009 called *Three Felonies a Day* by noted criminal lawyer Harvey A. Silverglate, with a foreward by Alan M. Dershowitz. The book convincingly explains what is happening in the system today, and cites a number of chilling real-life examples. And they point out that there is a very dangerous confluence of events now negatively affecting the criminal justice system in this country.

Between an explosion of statutes and laws on the books and the existence of onerous sentencing guidelines, the ability of prosecutors to hold lengthy sentences over the accused in order to negotiate a plea is producing a steep rise in negotiated pleas by those unwilling or unable to fight for their rights, push back, and go to trial, if necessary.

You don't have to look any further to prove this point than a recent case heard by the U. S. Supreme Court involving a fisherman in Florida being charged under Sarbanes Oxley for "obstruction of justice" for allegedly throwing four undersized fish overboard from his boat. The charge brought by zealous prosecutors carries a risk of substantial fines and up to 20 years in prison. The case awaits decision.

Mr. Petrocelli had gained much familiarity with the criminal justice system since his trip to Houston to defend Jeffrey Skilling and knew exactly how to game the system in Miami for his next client. He knew that if he could walk in and assert high enough damage numbers (no matter how false and fabricated) attributed to the FDI publication, and convince prosecutors of wrongdoing, then sentencing guidelines would allow the local prosecutors to hold the possibility of an astronomical sentence over Mr. Minkow's head to enhance the ability to negotiate a plea.

How would a prosecutor know that Mr. Petrocelli and Mr. Miller were gaming the US Attorney's office in order to remove Mr. Minkow from the playing field, and also gain an advantage in the coast to coast civil litigation vendetta brought by Lennar?

Sitting across from them were Mr. Miller, a local Miami businessman, and Petrocelli, who was a legend in his own mind (I got OJ!). Their story, like all great lies, sounded plausible on the surface. And they had the perfect guy to go after. Plus, Lennar's litigation vendetta had exhausted Mr. Minkow's and FDI's ability to defend against further attacks. So now was the time to pounce.

A post plea-bargain interview of Mr. Minkow in Lexington, Kentucky by former law enforcement officers revealed that he was forced into a plea specifically by the accusations and false representations made by Mr. Petrocelli and Mr. Miller to the Miami U.S. Attorney's office. The alleged dollar amounts of claimed damage to Lennar mattered a great deal and had a profound influence on the potential sentencing guidelines available to the Miami prosecutor.

And those damage claims are as false today as they were when made in the civil litigation arena, the criminal justice system, and various press releases.

Again, note the one place Lennar has not made these claims: in their Sarbanes-Oxley-governed filings with the SEC. And you can see why: we are talking about a lot more than four fish here. Which means they were comfortable lying to one branch of the government, the U.S. Attorneys in Miami, but not another, the SEC.

How can all of this criminal behavior be taking place in a public company? Good question, and this leads us to a discussion of how Lennar, while a public company, is actually structured and governed.

CHAPTER FOURTEEN

The Board of Mushrooms

LENNAR'S CAPITAL STRUCTURE consists of two classes of shares, A shares and B shares. The Miller family has a controlling block of B shares. This is good for them because B shares vote 10 to 1 to A shares, and the family has enough B shares to control every aspect of the company. Including the Lennar Board of Directors.

That is why Stuart Miller was able to ascend to become CEO when his father relinquished control without serious consideration of other viable candidates from within or outside the company.

Another great benefit of this capital structure, at least for Stuart Miller, was that the board of directors could be hand selected, compensation committees can be stacked, and Miller could now use the company as his personal piggybank, buy a jet, enrich his friends, and pursue personal agendas like the mindless squandering of enormous legal fees and costs to pursue a personal litigation vendetta.

Miller has directed Lennar to pay him outlandish amounts of money, far in excess of his peers in similar companies. In fact, in a recent survey contained in an article published in *The Wall Street Journal* on July 29, 2014, Miller topped the list of overpaid public builder chief executive officers. This is in spite of the fact that Lennar isn't near the top of the list in important metrics like return on equity.

And, based on their own testimony and actions (or inactions), the Lennar board members appear to have no idea about much of what the company is doing at the direction of Miller.

For example, Miller directed the company to spend huge sums of money in litigation fees and costs, tie up large blocks of executive time, and hire costly media spin companies. All of this directed at my company and me in an all-out litigation vendetta.

But the Lennar board members appeared to have no idea of the magnitude of these expenditures of money and time. There are a lot of companies far larger than Lennar ever will be that would have a laser focus on any matter that was draining off corporate resources to the tune of more than $100,000,000. Especially at a time when cash was king, queen, and the whole deck.

Here is testimony on the subject of litigation fees and costs taken in a deposition of director Kirk Landon on February 17, 2010:

Q. As you sit here today, do you have any idea what this litigation has cost Lennar?

A. Yes.

Q. And what's your sense of what —

A. Millions.

Q. Millions or tens of millions?

A. Millions is what I said.

Q. Is it your belief that it's cost less than $10 million?

A. No.

Q. Is it your view that it has cost more than $10 million?

A. Yes.

Q. Substantially more than $10 million?

A. I don't know.

Q. More than $50 million?

A. I doubt that.

Q. I think you might be surprised.

A. Pardon me.

Q. But you don't know the figure?

A. No.

And, on February 17, 2010, director Irving Bolotin testified:

Q. Do you know what Lennar has spent in connection with Mr. Marsch's litigations to-date?

A. No.

Q. Any idea?

A. No.

And worse, the board appears to have no idea that Miller was wrongfully enriching his friends at the expense of Lennar shareholders.

The whistleblower letter and our own discovery revealed that Stuart Miller was directing executives at Lennar to provide profit guarantees and no-loss guarantees to his personal friends involved in certain of Lennar's off-balance ventures. The whistleblower wrote:

> *"For example, Mr. Miller's friends, such as, Rony Seikely, have invested in multiple joint ventures, where Mr. Miller has verbally promised a guaranteed preferred return and/or no principal loss on his investment. Case in point: Mr. Seikely was an investor in 4 separate joint ventures during the height of the real estate frenzy. Mr. Miller ordered us to pay back Mr. Seikely and his company their principle and his guaranteed preferred return on one joint venture and the principal back on three other joint ventures. These four joint ventures are projected to incur significant losses and Mr. Miller chose to have Lennar shareholders take the losses, not Mr. Seikely."*

The only way Miller could conceal these activities was by avoiding reporting the true nature of these arrangements to the directors, stockholders, or the SEC. Can you now guess what was in the "black box"?

This blatant misuse of Lennar's assets is covered in detail in the next chapter recounting the Lakes deal steal, so there is no need for a thorough explanation here. But the evidence is overwhelming that Miller was directing Lennar executives to provide premium opportunities, sweetheart terms, and no-loss guarantees to his friends, like basketball player Rony Seikely. All at the expense of Lennar shareholders.

As the real estate markets continued to decline, Lennar shareholders took huge losses on venture interests acquired from Mr. Seikely and other friends of Miller. Where was the Board while this blatant and egregious siphoning of Lennar assets to Miller's friends was taking place?

We know where they were on at least one day in 2006. Lennar organized a helicopter tour in California for Board members in late June 2006. The tour included a fly-over of a few projects, but the centerpiece of the tour was the Bridges development.

On board the helicopter were directors R. Kirk Landon, Sidney Lapidus, Donna Shalala, and Jeffrey Sonnenfeld.

Jaffe stated at one point that the purpose of the helicopter tour was to *"Show the board what we could do."* This is the same Jaffe who repeatedly testified that under his direct supervision, the Bridges development "lost money" every day since Lennar assumed daily management. So, the point of the tour was to show the board they could lose money on literally anything?

So, buckle up, put on a recording of "Ride of the Valkyries", and let's imagine what the dialogue/travelogue might have been on this apocalyptic ride.

Board Member—*"This is a beautiful project, in fact I watched the televised golf matches here with Tiger Woods. This must be a very successful development."*

Lennar Tour Guide—*"Well, no. Actually it is complete failure. We wanted to show you where we have been squandering corporate resources and consistently losing Lennar's and our venture partner's money."*

Board Member—*"Does Mr. Miller know about this? How many more of these financial disasters are in our off-balance sheet portfolio?"*

Lennar Tour Guide—*"I don't know, but we will put our best and brightest on it immediately, and get the answer."*

This imaginary dialog didn't happen. What did happen was that the Board was shown Lennar's premier joint venture on the West Coast to reinforce to the Board how great everything was going and how capable the executives were. And they also took a five-minute detour after the Bridges fly-over to tour the Lakes development site.

No mention of the "losses" Jaffe testified to in depositions and on the witness stand. So, Jaffe was painting one picture for the Mushrooms, and a totally different one for me.

Just a few months after the triumphant helicopter tour in 2006, as real estate markets began to sour, Miller directed Lennar executives to bail out Mr. Seikely and his other friends, and set the table to shift heavy losses to the Lennar shareholders. There was no disclosure of that directive in any Lennar filing, and it is rather unlikely the Board was informed, either.

And also at this time Lennars' executives were scheming to set up the pensioners, savers, investors, and partners in a variety of ventures for aggregate losses well in excess of $1,000,000,000. They must not have been in Miller's friends and family plan.

One would hope the Board didn't know about these activities, but if they did, does that mean the Board was obligated to stand by and watch Stuart Miller enrich his friends at the expense of shareholders, to watch him squander unlimited funds on a personal litigation vendetta, and as he gamed and swindled virtually every one with whom Lennar does business? Who knows what else was going behind the Board's back?

Miller has been described in testimony by Board member Irving Bolotin as a *"first among equals"* on the Lennar Board. The concept of a *"first among equals"* is silly. Think about a horse race: at the starting line, all the horses are *"equal."* At the finish line, there is only one *"first."* *"First among equals"* is a politically polite way of saying Miller runs and dominates the Board. Just like the rest of the committees, including the Corporate Investment Committee (the CIC), and the compensation committee.

Regarding the letter I wrote to the Board in 2008, Lennar Board members testified that part of the job of a director was to receive communications through the reporting systems described above, and that letters, including complaints, were welcome.

Remarkably, instead of looking into the contents of my letter themselves, the board decided to hire a law firm to conduct an arms-length investigation of the allegations in the letter. Who did they hire? Mr. Petrocelli. Who was already deep in litigation with me and my company on behalf of Lennar, who was already regularly vacuuming Lennar's accounts to enrich his firm, and who was looking for another way to expand Miller's litigation vendetta.

This is exactly what happened at Enron when the chairman, Kenneth Lay, received information from Sherron Watkins, the Enron whistleblower. He directed the hiring of the Vinson & Elkins firm, a firm that was neck-deep in Enron's businesses, including the off-balance sheet entities, to investigate the allegations in Ms. Watkins memo. Not surprisingly, they didn't find any wrongdoing. But history tells us there was plenty of wrongdoing at Enron.

Hiring Petrocelli and his firm to investigate potential wrongdoing at Lennar was a waste of time and money. He wasn't part of the solution, he was part of the problem. And his job was to defend corporate criminals, not investigate them.

The letter simply provided another opportunity for Petrocelli to reach deeper into the Lennar shareholder pockets, open a new front for Miller's litigation vendetta, and step up the resource exhaustion tactics.

No board member appeared to have recommended or authorized a lawsuit in response to the letter, but Petrocelli and Miller began implementing a plan to file a lawsuit as quickly as possible. And they did.

Then the FDI Red Flags Report was released. As recounted before, Lennar immediately publically asserted that the company had been damaged to the tune of over $500,000,000. As indicated before, the Lennar Board met just four days after the publication of the report for a regularly scheduled meeting.

Lennar had released a response to the Red Flags Report just the day before the Board meeting. Since Miller and Petrocelli were feverishly preparing enormous "damage" claims tied to the decline in Lennar stock, you might think there would be extreme concern on the part of the Lennar Board and maybe even a little panic over the magnitude of the alleged "losses." $500,000,000 million bucks! *Iceberg! Get the lifeboats! We're sinking! Were doomed! Executives first! Women and children last!*

Nope. Not even close. Minutes of that Board meeting indicate that the Red Flags Report merited exactly two lines buried in a committee report, concluded nothing, and there was no mention of damage to the company of any kind. Much of the Board meeting was devoted to discussion of an amendment to the Equity Incentive Plan in order to further line the pockets of the Lennar key executives who were all present at the meeting, including Miller.

But, outside the Board's purview, Miller was privately going berserk over the Red Flags Report and the inside whistleblower's revelations. Miller understood the implications very well, and was opening the shareholder cash spigot for Petrocelli and his firm even further, and was getting ready to crank up at least two more Miami-based law firms.

But Miller did not appear to even bring the matter up to the Board except in a cursory way? One can only conclude Miller knew exactly what dangers the report and the letter presented, but wasn't about to be forthcoming about his concerns in the Board meeting.

The events described in this chapter support the premise that this was truly a Board that simply had no idea of what was really going on in regard to Miller's costly litigation vendetta and the real reasons behind it. Nor did they appear to know that Miller was enriching his friends at Lennar shareholder expense. But hey, as long as the directors' fee checks keep coming in on time, what's the problem?

This company has no real checks and balances or real governance other than Miller. And speaking of Miller, that takes us to the Miller and Jaffe - orchestrated Lakes project deal steal.

CHAPTER FIFTEEN

The Deal Steal

PERHAPS NO SINGLE transaction, LandSource excepted, illustrates the sheer dishonesty of Lennar, its executives, and its lawyers better than their interaction with my company and me on a development project known as the Lakes at Rancho Santa Fe.

According to the terms of our agreement with Lennar to co-develop the Bridges golf and residential community, any similar residential development opportunity that became available within the market area was designated as a "Company Opportunity."

A development opportunity similar to the Bridges was in fact presented to us, and Jaffe and I decided to jointly pursue the opportunity on behalf of our Bridges development company. The Lakes was located just a mile or so from the Bridges development, of similar terrain, and in a very good location. In a deposition taken on January 23, 2007, Jaffe testified:

Q. Mr. Jaffe, it's true that you first learned about the McCrink Ranch (The Lakes) real estate development opportunity from Nick Marsch, correct?

A. Correct.

An agreement to pursue the opportunity on behalf of our jointly-owned development company was reached by me with Jaffe and Lennar. My role as co-developer was to negotiate terms with the seller and manage the acquisition of the project on behalf of either our existing Bridges development company or a new specific-purpose LLC.

Jaffe further testified:

Q. Well, it's true that the two of you agreed together to go after acquiring and developing the McCrink Ranch (The Lakes) real estate development, correct?

A. I'm sorry. I just want to make sure I understand your question clearly. Yes, we — Nick and I pursued the — the property together. In fact, Nick took the lead in — in the pursuit of the property.

Q. Your agreement with Mr. Marsch was the two of you would work together to obtain and exploit the McCrink Ranch (The Lakes) real estate development opportunity, correct?

A. I think that's a fair characterization.

Q. Okay. And then the two of you worked together, like you worked together with the Bridges, to try to capture that opportunity on behalf of the two of you, correct?

A. Mr. Marsch and I worked together on the pursuit and the control of the McCrink property (The Lakes).

The Lakes was a relatively large development project, with over 350 luxury homesites and special access rights to an existing adjacent golf course, called the Crosby. And it was potentially a very profitable opportunity.

Managing the acquisition of this development was an arduous process, taking almost two years. There were numerous starts and stops in the process, dead ends and obstacles, a dysfunctional selling group to manage, but finally we reached an agreement with the seller on the terms of a purchase and the transaction was set to close in February of 2006.

It was well worth the time and effort expended to acquire the Lakes project. The opportunity was the last large developable parcel in Rancho Santa Fe. Building permits were in place, the negotiated terms reduced go-forward risk, and the profit projections were very good.

In the Lennar executives' own words obtained from internal memoranda:

"A wonderful opportunity to build high-end homes on one of the last great undeveloped land opportunities in North San Diego County."

And we had the "brought to you by the developers of the Bridges" cachet working for us, as well.

But, as always happens when dealing with Lennar and Jaffe, something happened on the way to bank, just like it did with the Bridges project.

At the closing of the Lakes acquisition on February 7, 2006, Lennar switched the buyer to a secretly-formed partnership with one of Stuart Miller's Miami friends, Rony

Seikely, a former basketball player, and his land investment fund called Quadrant.

In fact, Lennar, on Miller's orders, had already secretly conveyed the highly profitable development opportunity to his friend Seikely and Quadrant months earlier, but kept that fact to themselves while I continued the negotiation process on behalf of our jointly-owned development company.

On January 23, 2007 Jaffe testified:

Q. Did Lennar, to your knowledge, ever communicate to Mr. Marsch prior to February 7, 2006 that it was going to exclude him from the acquisition of McCrink Ranch (The Lakes)?

A. I'm not aware of that.

Q. Did you ever disclose to Mr. Marsch . . . that Mr. Seikely was good friends with Mr. Miller?

A. I don't think I ever discussed Mr. Seikely with Mr. Marsch prior to closing.

Q. So the answer is you never disclosed his (Seikely) relationship with Mr. Miller, true?

A. Never discussed anything about Mr. Seikely with Mr. Marsch prior to closing. Not that I can recall.

Yet Lennar had executed an agreement with Seikely/Quadrant months before the closing at the instigation of Miller, and usurped the opportunity from our jointly-owned development company to benefit one of Miller's personal friends.

Jaffe testified on January 25, 2007 that Miller *"did want us to try to grow the relationship with Mr. Seikely and find deals that were a good opportunities and a good fit for him."*

A Lennar executive, Emile Haddad, wrote an email to Mr. Seikely: *"I just wanted to make sure to find the perfect deal for you."*

And Seikely said to his investors about the Lakes: *"these kinds of great deals are reserved for close relationships and thus would not be available otherwise."*

The whistleblower letter I received provided information about Mr. Miller and his friend Seikely that tied 100% with information gathered through the litigation discovery process. The letter said:

> *For example, Mr. Miller's friends, such as, Rony Seikely, have invested in multiple joint ventures, where Mr. Miller has verbally promised a guaranteed preferred return and/or no principal loss on his investment. Case in point: Mr. Seikely was an investor in 4 separate joint ventures during the height of the real estate frenzy. Mr. Miller ordered us to pay back Mr. Seikely and his company their principal and his guaranteed preferred return on one joint venture and the principal back on three other joint ventures. These four joint ventures are projected to incur significant losses and Mr. Miller chose to have Lennar shareholders take the losses, not Mr. Seikely.*

Only when confronted after Lennar surreptitiously switched buyers and obtained title did Jaffe inform me that

Lennar had planned for months to exclude me and my company from the Lakes development opportunity in favor of Miller's friend Seikely and his Quadrant fund. And that my company and I were excluded from this $800,000,000 development opportunity. This is after not only my bringing the opportunity to our jointly-owned Bridges development company, as our agreement required, but also after I spent two years and countless hours negotiating the transaction on behalf of our venture.

Think about this: Lennar and Jaffe have taken the position that the Bridges development "has lost money" from inception and has never turned a profit. But they schemed and connived to steal the Lakes opportunity from our jointly-owned Bridges development company. Was that because they enjoyed losing money, and wanted to share the experience with Miller's friend Seikely in a similar development just a five minute drive from the Bridges?

This "deal steal" led, of course, to a dispute over our exclusion from this lucrative development opportunity. It wasn't just that Jaffe's word is no good, bad enough to be sure, it's that he actively lied and misled, as well. It's the Lennar Way.

Eventually, as the specter of litigation loomed, Jaffe made a few desultory offers to settle the matter. The first offer was to "split profits" on the Lakes development.

Sure — just like the profit split in our Bridges development. Profits? We couldn't even get an honest accounting of our capital contribution, much less recognition or payment of the Bridges profits interest. Let me tell you this: if you are in an arrangement that involves a profit split with

Lennar, don't wait by the mailbox for the check.

This profit split offer, made in late 2006, was from the very same Jaffe that was running out of excuses on the Bridges accounting and then testified that "we've lost money every day for 10 years" on the Bridges development! What profits? It wasn't hard to visualize Lennar loading up their pigs at the trough at the Bridges and trucking them five minutes away to the Lakes development.

Next, Jaffe came up with a "back-end" participation offer. Let me put it this way: If Lennar offers you a "back-end" interest in anything, and you are inclined to have a professional assist you in analyzing the proposal, then hire a proctologist. Don't waste your money on a lawyer or financial advisor. And don't wait by the mailbox on this one, either.

Clearly an illusory profit split or a "back-end" interest with Lennar was of no interest to me, but negotiations to resolve the situation continued. No realistic offers were made by Lennar, no agreement was reached, and litigation was filed in late 2006. We appropriately moved to tie up the Lakes property until a fair and equitable resolution was reached.

Lennar, of course, had their usual army of lawyers handle this case, along with the Bridges accounting and conversion case. And all of the expected tactics were utilized: creation of phony evidentiary issues, character assassination, endless depositions laced with trick questions designed, as always, to mislead the deponent and ultimately a trier of fact. And the case was assigned to the same judge as the Bridges case.

DESPITE THE OVERWHELMING proof that Lennar had stolen the Lakes opportunity, the in-over-his-head Bridges trial judge, who was also assigned the Lakes case, dismissed the case on the eve of trial based on highly misleading papers filed by Petrocelli and his team.

By that time the judge was clearly unable or unwilling to deal with the torrent of motions, hearings, fabricated evidentiary issues, and out-and-out lies presented to him by Petrocelli and the rest of the Lennar lawyers. The judge was rubber-stamping anything they put in front of him. With a stroke of the pen he could make the case go away. And did. This did not portend a fair hearing in the upcoming Bridges trial.

An appeal of the judge's Lakes case ruling was, of course, filed immediately. The appellate court not-so-politely disagreed with the trial judge, as they often do, and reversed the trial court judge's ruling in a resounding 29 page unanimous opinion. Here are quotes from that opinion:

> "Our thorough review of Marsch's deposition compels us to agree with Briarwood"
>
> "Lennar agreed to pursue the McCrink Ranch (The Lakes) development jointly with Briarwood" . . . then Lennar manipulated the negotiations with the McCrink family so that the legal right to acquire the McCrink Ranch (The Lakes) property was documented in the name of a Lennar affiliate; secretly nego-

tiated with another person to enter into agreement to acquire the McCrink Ranch (The Lakes) property via an entity that excluded Briarwood; formed Rancho Santa Fe Lakes Partners, LLC for the express purpose of acquiring the McCrink Ranch (The Lakes), joined with Quadrant San Diego, LLC (Rony Seikely) to squeeze out Briarwood and usurp the McCrink Ranch (The Lakes) property; and misled Briarwood about its intent to exclude it from the McCrink Ranch (The Lakes) opportunity."

Lennar did not appeal this order. You might think it was over as far as Lennar's lawyers trying to simply fool a judge into signing another Where-do-I-sign order on this case. If you thought that, you would be wrong. In fact, as highlighted in the beginning of this chapter, Lennar and their dishonest lawyers were just getting started.

Since Lennar didn't fare well in the California appellate court on this case, they filed a new claim in Miami, Florida, loosely based on the case, but with a new twist that was a perfect example of the Petrocelli alternate universe approach to litigation: they were now the victims, and we were the bad guys.

THE LEGAL SYSTEM in Miami works in strange and interesting ways. There is a constant revolving door be-

tween the bench and private practice. Today's judge is tomor-
rows' advocate and vice versa. And prospective judges run for
office, raise funds in substantial amounts, and must take care
not to offend their contributors. Not surprisingly, law firms
and lawyers comprise a good portion of the donor base for
these campaigns. It is understood that if a judge is kind and
benevolent to upper and top-tier law firms and their clients,
then a job will be waiting at the end of their stint on the bench.

Lennar's primary local litigation counsel in Miami is a former judge, David Gersten, one of the Gersten brothers. His
brother Joe, also a lawyer (until he was disbarred by the Florida
Supreme Court), fled the country amid charges involving pros-
titution, drug use, and car theft.

Nobody epitomized the revolving door like Mr. Gersten.
Once a circuit court judge, then an appellate judge, and now
in private practice representing Lennar. Perfect.

There was a hearing on November 5, 2013 in Miami involving the Florida case filed by Lennar, and in pre-hearing
banter, the sitting judge referred to attorney Gersten as
"Judge" Gersten. And it became obvious very quickly that
there was more than one "judge" actually running this hearing. Although fortunately I had once been invited to judge a
bikini contest, nobody called me "Judge" at the hearing.

So Lennar simply moved the litigation party to Miami
and filed a lawsuit in their own backyard actually accusing us
of interfering with their deal with Miller's pal Seikely and his
Quadrant Fund. You know — the deal that Jaffe testified
had been actively concealed from me so I would continue
to move the acquisition to the finish line for our jointly-
owned company.

This interference allegedly was a causation of damages to Lennar when Miller directed Lennar to buy out his friend Seikely at an above market price, thereby insuring Seikely's profit, but then this overpayment virtually guaranteed that Lennar, meaning its shareholders, would take a loss on the property. And they did. To claim that this loss was attributable to my company and me was utterly preposterous, but all in a day's work for Petrocelli and company.

So in this case, Lennar is like a bank robber who robs the bank, flees with a bag of money, drives to the nearest casino, puts the money on the pass line, loses every dime, and then sues the bank for the loss.

The new Miami claim was remarkable in its deceptiveness and its fraudulent nature:

- It failed to mention the history of the Lakes acquisition.
- It failed to mention the surreptitious "deal-steal" from our jointly-owned company in favor of Miller's personal friend.
- It failed to mention the clear appellate ruling in California identifying Lennar as *"manipulating" "misleading" and "usurping"* the Lakes opportunity.
- It failed to mention that the eventual Lennar acquisition of the Lakes property interest from Seikely/Quadrant was but one of four above-market bailouts of Seikely and Millers' friends to the detriment of Lennar stockholders.
- It failed to mention that Millers friend Seikely couldn't follow through with contractual funding obligations, trig-

gering the acquisition of Quadrant's interest.

   • It failed to mention that Seikely and his investors were spooked by the rapid downturn in the market and wanted out.

   • It failed to mention that Miller directed Lennar executives to buy his friends out at a profit in a declining market.

   • It failed to mention that Lennar used the Lakes property to obtain a huge tax refund with a sham sale, yet maintained control of the property, while mitigating losses with taxpayer money.

Lennar has a committee called the Corporate Investment Committee or, for short, CIC. Jaffe testified about how the committee actually functions in his deposition January 23, 2007:

   Q. Okay. But above Jon Jaffe, the only person or entity that needs to give you authority to buy something like McCrink Ranch (The Lakes) is CIC, correct?

   A. I believe above a certain dollar amount, CIC would have to get approval from the company's CEO.

   Q. And the company's CEO is who?

   A. Stuart Miller.

So it's not too difficult to divine that the CIC operates at the whim of — guess who — Stuart Miller.

   We obtained a copy of an internal Lennar memo addressed to the CIC, aka Miller, from a Lennar executive named Mike Levesque. The stated subject of the memo is:

   "Rancho Santa Fe Partners (Seikely)—Quadrant Membership

Interest Purchase."

And in the first part of the memo is an executive summary. And here is what it reads:

> "Lennar Homes of California, Inc. "Lennar") is pursuing a strategy in which it will purchase the membership interest (the "interest") of Quadrant San Diego, LLC ("Quadrant") (collectively the "members") in Rancho Santa Fe Lakes Partners, LLC (the "company"). This decision is predicated on Quadrant's inability to fund additional capital to the Venture, the Fin 46 accounting consequences of Lennar having to fund the additional capital and the conclusion that the asset can be best managed in the near term with Lennar in complete control of the asset management strategy."

And the memo goes on to state:

"It is also felt, if Lennar was the only member putting in additional capital, it should get the benefit of any upside on the project."

In other words, Mr. Seikely's fund, Quadrant, was unable or unwilling to provide additional capital to the venture, and Lennar was "pursuing a strategy" to gain "complete control of the asset", and Lennar could get "the benefit of any upside on the project.", with a negotiated buyout. This was a voluntary transaction in all respects, and Lennar was not being forced to do anything. In fact, as usual, Lennar had a plan all along, as is evidenced by the Levesque memo to the Corporate Investment Committee.

And the CIC memo goes into a brief discussion of our perfectly valid deal-steal claims regarding the Lakes, but the only real problem was that Miller's pal Seikely wasn't prepared or may not have been capable of raising or investing more money in the property. And by then, Miller had directed Lennar to bail Seikely and his friends out at a profit in not one, but four failing investments with Lennar.

Why is that? Well, thanks to Quadrant's investor website, we have the answer. There were four land deals between Quadrant and Lennar. The Lakes was just one of them. According to Quadrant's website Lennar bought out all four positions, giving a 100% return of capital and a profit on all of the deals. All voluntary and consensual transactions. In other words, Quadrant had no legal ability whatsoever to demand a buyout or payoff, especially at a profit in each deal. And Lennar didn't have an obligation to buy out the positions, either. At any price, much less at a profit.

The Seikely/Quadrant website displayed a document entitled "Portfolio." In this publicly disseminated document, Quadrant Investment Group disclosed exactly why and how its interest in the Lakes was acquired by Lennar:

"In February, 2007 Lennar made an offer to buy out Quadrant San Diego's joint venture interest, and for the reasons stated in Quadrant I above, the offer was accepted and in 2007 each member of Quadrant San Diego received 100% of their investment plus a profit"

Here are the publically stated reasons for the Lennar

buyout offer:

"In January 2007 they (Lennar) made an offer to buy out Quad-rant I's joint venture interest. Given the serious recent depression of the new home construction industry and it's negative impact on land values, Quadrant I entertained Lennar's offer and as a result in 2007 all members of Quadrant I received 100% of their invest-ment plus a profit."

No mention whatsoever of a legal dispute in Rancho Santa Fe, and, in any event, such a dispute would have nothing whatsoever to do with the other three above-market buy-outs of Quadrant positions by Lennar. And at least one of these buy-outs preceded the Lakes buyout.

As an aside, note this: the buyout offer comes to Quadrant in January of 2007. And even the basketball player notes that there is a "serious recent depression of the new home construction industry and its negative impact on land values." Jaffe and Miller didn't know this when they leveraged LandSource two months later using phony ap-praisals and cash flows and put it on an inevitable path to bankruptcy?" Of course they did.

The whistleblower letter I received in November 2008 specifically addressed the Lennar, Miller, and Seikely situation with uncanny accuracy. The letter writer stated:

> *. . . The fact is the joint venture part-ners are personal friends of Stuart Miller. For example, Mr. Miller's friends, such as Rony Seikely, have in-*

vested in multiple joint ventures, where Mr. Miller has verbally promised a guaranteed preferred return and/or no principal loss on his investment. Case in point: Mr. Seikely was an investor in 4 separate joint ventures during the height of the real estate frenzy. Mr. Miller ordered us to pay back Mr. Seikely and his company their principal and his guaranteed preferred return on one joint venture, and the principal back on three other joint ventures. These four joint ventures are projected to incur significant losses and Mr. Miller chose to have Lennar shareholders take the losses, not Mr. Seikely.

And that is exactly what happened. Which proved that the letter writer knew exactly what he or she was talking about.

There is also ample evidence that Miller was directing personal friends to invest with Seikely in his funds, so now he was going to rescue them from potential disaster by bailing out all of Seikely's Quadrant funds at a profit amid a rapidly declining market. And the Lennar shareholders ultimately bore huge losses as a result.

And the Miller/Seikely personal relationship was very close: in a deposition taken on September 12, 2008, Miller testified:

Q. Do you travel socially with Mr. Seikely?
A. Yes . . . we are friends, we have traveled socially.

Q. Have you ever double dated with Mr. Seikely?

A. Oh, yeah.

Q. Okay, can you estimate how many times . . . ?

A. Let's say it's probably more than 10 times.

Let's go back to Lennar executive Michael Levesque. He wrote an email to the Lennar Lakes acquisition team shortly before they hijacked the Lakes development opportunity and he was complaining about the sky-high cost of doing business with Miller's friend Seikely. He stated that the deal would *"cost us an additional almost $6 million."* And other Lennar execs internally complained that *"Seikely/Quadrant is taking advantage of Lennar through high-return investments costing Lennar millions more than other alternatives"*, but that the executives are powerless to stop this diversion of project revenues due to *"political implications."*

By the way, *"political implications"* simply means "don't interfere with Stuart Miller's machinations with his friends", even if the Lennar shareholders are getting robbed.

And Lennar has spent untold millions on this baseless lawsuit it filed against my company and me in Miami, accusing us of causing "losses" in connection with the Lakes transaction. This lawsuit led to the Kafkaesque trial on December 2, 2013 recounted in Chapter 16.

Petrocelli put Lennar's CFO, Bruce Gross, on the witness stand as their principal witness to testify regarding the "losses" suffered by Lennar after they voluntarily decided to bail out Mr. Seikely from his Quadrant Fund's investment with Lennar in the Lakes development.

After blathering for a while about Lennar's integrity, Mr. Gross, another coached Lennar liar, when questioned by

Petrocelli in front of the jury about the reason Lennar acquired Quadrant's interest in the Lakes development, testified:

*"So what we did is we decided it wasn't fair to our partner
(Seikely), and we bought out our partner's interest, their 75%, because
that property wasn't going to go forward, and we bought them out,
and then we figured we would just deal with Marsch ourselves."*

Mr. Gross's duplicitous testimony was wholly inaccurate and deceptive. Another proud Petrocelli pupil. Compare this concocted and wholly misleading testimony to the
indisputable facts documented in this chapter.

Even if there was an issue about us pursuing legitimate
deal steal claims regarding the Lakes development, how did
that explain why Lennar, at the same time, was methodically acquiring Quadrant's interests in four separate, distinct, and geographically diverse land deals, and at
above-market prices in all cases? And at a profit in a failing
and declining market.

Returning to Mr. Gross's disingenuous testimony about
"fairness", being "fair" had nothing to do with the
Seikely/Quadrant buyout (and let's get serious, the word
"fairness" isn't in the Lennar dictionary). The buyout was
driven by Stuart Miller bailing out his pal Seikely and
Miller's friends who had invested with him in the Quadrant funds. And Lennar continued to go forward with the
development without interruption or pause.

That this buy-out arrangement had nothing to do with
"fairness" is proven conclusively by deposition testimony
given by Jaffe on January 25, 2007 concerning other buy-

outs by Lennar occurring at exactly the same time as the Quadrant transactions.

Jaffe testified:

Q. Are you (Lennar) buying out any investors other than Mr. Seikely's fund?

A. Yes.

Q. Who?

A. RFC.

Q. And how many transactions?

A. . . . I believe there's eight transactions.

And he goes on to explain why they are buying out RFC:

Q. Why then are you buying out their investment?

A. As I just said to you, there is a rapidly changing market. This particular case, we've got a very good relationship with them. They invested in the transaction because of the relationship. It wasn't something they really wanted to do, but they did it because they felt it was important to the relationship and important to us. Things haven't worked out well. And we're working it out with them.

Q. First, are they getting all the capital back?

A. The vast majority of it.

Q. Are they getting a return on their capital?

A. I do not believe they are getting a return on their capital.

So another investor, RFC, is getting a haircut on capital invested and no return at the same time Lennar is buying Seikely/Quadrant's multiple interests out on above-market terms at a profit even though Jaffe testified in regard to

RFC that *"we've got a very good relationship with them."*

"Things haven't worked out well" seems to be very good description of anything Jaffe touches (at least for the unsuspecting victim).

And it gets worse: Mr. Levesque indicated in the Quadrant Membership Purchase Memo that RFC was another investor in the Lakes transaction. RFC and Quadrant were both invested with Lennar in the Lakes transaction. RFC, with whom Jaffe testified Lennar has a *very good relationship*, was losing substantial money while Miller's friend Seikely was being bought out at a profit!

Like the whistleblower said, *"it pays to be a friend of Stuart Miller."* RFC must not have been invited to double date with Miller.

So, back to Mr. Gross and his heart-rending "fairness" testimony. Was it was fair to let me bring the Lakes deal to our venture, agree to pursue it jointly, let me do the arduous acquisition work, actively conceal their real intentions, and then steal it from our venture and secretly give it to Millers' friend on terms injurious to Lennar shareholders?

And then was it "fair" to sue my company and me asserting frivolous, baseless, and meritless claims, spending tens of millions of shareholder dollars in a further attempt to exhaust our resources and make us go away and stop asking for our money back? Fairness? Get serious.

The next chapter takes a look at how Petrocelli and Lennar cynically undermined the foundation of our legal system to fraudulently obtain a huge verdict, the sham trial in Miami on December 2, 2013.

CHAPTER SIXTEEN

The Florida Billion Dollar Verdict

THERE ARE THREE very high stakes cases making the news recently that have striking similarities. All three involve a sophisticated fraud on the court by plaintiff's lawyers and their clients. And all three involve false and ghostwritten expert testimony among other tactics. And all three involve cynical and wholesale subversion of the legal system by dishonest plaintiffs' lawyers and their equally dishonest clients.

Meritless cases have been transformed into multibillion dollar verdicts by overt, calculated wholesale fraud on the courts. These cases have dragged on for years and have consumed millions of dollars in legal fees and costs for the wrongfully accused defendants.

A *USA Today* story on April 16, 2014 entitled "Big Legal Battles, Bigger Lies" summed up two of the cases quite nicely. And the final outcome of both cases was total vindication for the wrongly accused defendants, but not before reputations were tarnished, many millions of dollars were spent on defense of these meritless claims, and pressures were brought to settle the fabricated claims for billions of dollars.

The largest case is Chevron v. Donziger and involved the use of a rigged expert witness by plaintiffs' lawyers who engaged in a fraud on the court to obtain a very large judgment. The core of the plaintiff's lawyers' wrongdoing was co-opting a supposed "independent" expert witness and influencing and ghost-writing his reports to the court. And there were allegations of judicial misconduct as well. As a result of these machinations, the court found in the plaintiff's favor to the tune of $19,000,000,000 against Chevron.

The next case involved Dole Foods being sued for billions of dollars by plaintiffs' lawyers on behalf of Nicaraguan agricultural workers over alleged harmful chemical exposure. The lawyers allegedly submitted false expert reports, false medical reports, coached witnesses to lie, and provided other contrived testimony to the court. Their unconscionable conduct was ultimately ruled a "fraud on the court." The case was thrown out upon discovery of the attempted fraud on the court by an astute judge in Los Angeles, CA.

These cases started with superficially plausible but false allegations followed by "independent" expert opinions retro-engineered to support the made-up charges. And in the Chevron case the judge's orders and punitive verdict were actually written by scheming plaintiffs' lawyers.

The third case involves exactly the same conduct by plaintiffs' lawyers and their clients plus even more egregious behavior. My company and I are the defendants and victims in this case. We have also had to incur millions of dollars in ruinous legal fees and costs to try to defend against false allegations brought by Lennars' corporate executives and their lawyers. And have borne the brunt of ceaseless media barrages designed to inflict reputational damage and enhance the other side's character assassination strategy.

And virtually every tactic used by the plaintiffs' lawyers in the Chevron and Dole cases have been employed in our case: fabricated allegations supported by false and ghost-written expert opinions, witnesses coached to lie, the preparation and signature of where-do-I-sign orders by compliant judges, and even documented judicial misconduct.

The Chevron v. Donziger case is the subject of a book recently published by author and journalist Paul M. Barrett called *Law of the Jungle*. The parallels to what occurred in the Chevron case and the amazingly similar conduct by Lennar and its lawyers in our case are astonishing. The culmination of Lennar and its counsel's five-year effort to defraud the court, assert baseless and frivolous claims, and obtain punitive judgments against us played out in a made-for-a-movie trial on December 2, 2013 in a Miami courtroom.

Lennar engineered an uncontested judgment against my company and me for more than $1,000,000,000. One billion dollars!

Why uncontested? A Miami circuit court judge, John Thornton, and his predecessor, Jose Rodriguez, were induced to sign a series of punitive orders based on manufactured and unsupportable legal claims combined with fraudulent "expert" testimony. These orders denied due process, denied counsel, suspended constitutional rights, and prohibited us from participating whatsoever in the trial process. And that was the idea.

And even more shocking, all of the court orders signed without change by Judge Thornton and his predecessor judge were written and submitted by Lennar lawyers. Who exactly was running the courtroom?

Here, in black and white, is just one of the judge's rulings:

"Defendant Nicolas Marsch III is hereby precluded from contesting Lennar's damages evidence during the trial on the matter. Defendant Marsch will not be permitted to present any evidence at the damages trial, or contest any evidence presented by Lennar."

The judge had already issued a similar order regarding my company, Briarwood Capital LLC. And in companion orders, the judge, de facto, denied availability of counsel, and then promptly scheduled a farcical one-sided trial in the matter.

So, according to this judge's orders, due process and constitutional rights were suspended, there was no rule of law in force, and the defendants were denied counsel, would not be permitted to speak, participate, present evidence, argue, or contest evidence. Welcome to Miami.

So what would be the point of either defendant attending this farce in Miami?

The Dec 2, 2013 courtroom scene was something right out of a Grisham novel.

The trial was convened at 9:27 am in Miami and the charade began. Mr. Petrocelli and several additional lawyers from his firm appeared on behalf of Lennar, as well as a number of Miami lawyers. And, of course, several Lennar executives came for the show, including Stuart Miller and his usual highly-paid entourage, which included Lennar's general counsel, Mark Sustana.

Judge Thornton stated on the record that:

"Mr. Marsch is not here. He has, in my humble opinion, elected at this stage not to be here."

"Elected" not to be here? What? You mean he didn't want to fly three thousand miles to Miami and be tied to a chair with a bag over his head like a Taliban prisoner?

And the charade continued as the judge, at Petrocelli's direction, set up the proceeding for a one-sided jury trial. If one-sided wasn't unfair enough, the process undertaken by plaintiffs' counsel to mislead and deceive the prospective jury pool about why the defendants weren't present was breathtaking. Amazingly, the judge actively participated with Petrocelli in the process of misleading jurors. Fortunately, it is on the record for all to see.

As the proceedings unfolded, Mr. Petrocelli and the judge never informed jurors that the defendants were *court-ordered* not to speak, participate, contest evidence, or present evidence in defense of Lennar's false claims. Nor were jurors told that the judge had de facto denied counsel to the defendants.

Here is the legal definition of the word trial: "a formal examination of evidence before a judge, and typically a jury,

in order to decide guilt in a case of criminal or civil proceedings." A court order precluding one side from presentation of evidence, or contesting evidence presented by the
other side, is a de-facto denial of due process. All other aspects of the trial process are merely procedural.

Here are some direct quotes taken from the trial transcript
of statements made by the trial judge and Mr. Petrocelli acting in concert to mislead jurors. There were highly pertinent
due process questions asked by prospective jurors, who were
then further misled, admonished not to think, and then summarily dismissed.

These quotes are taken verbatim from the court transcript
of the vital jury selection process and clearly show that every
effort is made to conceal the true nature of the proceedings
from prospective jurors and to make it look like my company and I simply decided ("elected") not to show up and
"participate." And that my company and I could have appeared and defended Lennar's baseless accusations if we so
chose.

As you review these quotes made in the trial and jury selection process, keep in mind my company and I are specifically barred by the judge's own orders from participating in
the process in any way, including making opening or closing
statements that would in any way present or contest evidence,
contesting alleged and unproven damage claims, and cross-
examining witnesses. We were court-ordered not to present
evidence, including expert reports and testimony which
would have easily proved Lennar's claims were baseless (and
they were). Gagged and bound. And if my company and I
had counsel appearing on our behalf, the same rules applied.

Here are verbatim quotes from Mr. Petrocelli, the judge, and prospective jurors:

Judge Thornton—*"Good morning. We're here in the matter of Lennar vs. Briarwood, Case No. 08-55741"* . . .

Judge Thornton—*"Mr. Marsch is not here. He has, in my humble opinion, elected at this stage not to be here."*

Mr. Petrocelli—*"So it is clear to us that he has elected not to appear."*

(Prospective jurors enter the room)

Judge Thornton—*"Mr. Marsch . . . has made a decision, on his own, that he is not going to participate in these proceedings."*

The definition of the word participate is: *"to take part in, to engage in, to share in, to join in, play a part in, partake in, be a participant in."*

Did this judge bother to read the order written for him by Lennar's lawyers that he signed without change? How could he make this statement in good faith? Participate?

Judge Thornton—*". . . as I've explained to you, that neither Mr. Marsch or Briarwood are here or are represented by lawyers."*

Since the judge signed another order written for him by Lennar's lawyers (and again signed without change) that effectively prevented counsel from representing me, the part about no lawyers representing the defendants couldn't have been too much of a surprise to him.

Mr. Petrocelli—*"Mr. Marsch and Briarwood were given no-*

tice of this trial against them, but they have elected not to appear."

Mr. Petrocelli—*"Mr. Marsch elected not to have counsel here today, and not to appear himself, as he had the right to do. So, we are here and you are here without having to hear from Mr. Marsch, but that was his choice and his decision."*

Mr. Petrocelli — *". . . Mr. Marsch had the opportunity to come and present his side of the case with or without lawyers and elected not to do so."*

Present his side of the case? By what means? Hand puppets?

Mr. Petrocelli — *"Here we are here and here they are (the jury) and here he is not. And that is not our decision. That's his choice."*

And the judge sat and listened to Mr. Petrocelli lie repeatedly to jurors without saying a word. And then the judge even chimed in with his own misleading statements to the jury. Not once had the judge informed the jury pool that he had directly ordered that my company and I were not to participate in the process in any way.

But many of the prospective jurors were troubled by the proceeding and asked why there weren't two sides to this story for the jury to hear. Their questions were met with more misleading statements:

Mr. Petrocelli—*"Now you heard from the court that Mr. Marsch made a decision not to appear here today . . . he made a decision not to have a lawyer and not to show up here. Is anyone here going to hold that against Lennar because Mr. Marsch decided not to come here or have a lawyer here today?*

Prospective Juror:— *"What do you mean by hold against? Because I'm naturally going to have some questions about why he shouldn't show up, so I'm going to question those motives."*

Petrocelli— *"Unfortunately I can't answer that question because I don't know why he didn't show up . . . He was given notice to appear and has made a decision not to appear, and my concern is that no one on the jury is to speculate as to those reasons and hold that against the company (Lennar) . . . I really need to know that because you wouldn't be a suitable person to be sitting on the jury . . .*

Then the court chimes in:

Judge Thornton . . . *So I really can't — I don't want you speculating that — or doing anything with that other than just knowing that he decided not to be here."*

In other words, the prospective jurors were admonished by both Mr. Petrocelli and the judge not to think, not to question the absurdity of the proceedings, not to raise or even consider due process issues, and to blindly accept the misrepresentations by the court and the plaintiffs' lawyers. Don't even think about thinking.

But members of the jury pool continued to probe for the real reason why this was a one-sided trial, and the misrepresentations and calculated admonishments continued throughout the jury selection process.

Another Prospective Juror—*"We can't hear both sides? I'm sorry if I missed that part. So we can hear the situation of both sides and try to figure out the whole entire case?" I don't know if you . . . This* prospective juror is cut off in mid-question by Mr. Petrocelli who said:

Petrocelli—"*Yes, I'm glad you asked that question. We are here to present our side of the case, and Mr. Marsch had the opportunity to come and present his side of the case with or without lawyers and elected not to do so.*"

Petrocelli—"*This was his obligation or . . . if he wanted to do so.*"

Mr. Petrocelli—"*He will not be here apparently, unless he shows up, to present any evidence.*"

In the presence of all of the prospective jurors, Petrocelli responded to the juror's very pertinent question with an unqualified lie. Any prospective juror who raised a due process concern was summarily rejected. He knew for an absolute certainty that the court order specifically precluded presentation of any evidence in that court room other than the bogus "evidence" obtained from Lennar's coached and scripted witnesses.

The judge sat mutely and allowed these thoroughly false and misleading statements to be made in his courtroom without correction, without admonishment, and with his full cooperation. His conduct was inexplicable.

And it wasn't just the judge who sat, listened, and participated in these lies being put on the record.

Stuart Miller was in attendance at the trial. He listened to his lawyer lie repeatedly throughout the jury selection process and the trial itself. And in case there is any doubt that Miller fully understood what was going on in the proceedings, let's put that to rest by noting that Mr. Miller has a law degree from Harvard. Plus he had Lennar's general counsel sitting by his side at the proceedings.

Miller knew exactly what was going on in that courtroom. He knew that Lennar and its lawyers were systematically undermining the justice system, just as he and Petrocelli knew they were doing the same in their duplicitous visits and letters to the nearby U.S. Attorneys' office.

Sitting with Miller in the courtroom was David Gersten, former circuit court judge, former appellate judge, and now Lennar's local face to the court and thumb on the scales of justice in Miami.

It was Mr. Gersten and the rest of the Lennar lawyers who had supplied the Where-Do-I-Sign orders to judge Thornton and his predecessor denying due process and effectively denying counsel. He was also involved in preparing and submitting the fraudulent ghost-written expert reports to the court that were the basis of those punitive orders. The expert reports are discussed in detail in the next chapter.

Did Mr. Gersten, former judge, jump up and interrupt the proceedings, admonish his colleague and co-counsel Mr. Petrocelli to stop lying to prospective jurors, stop undermining the all-important jury system, and suggest the judge do the same? If you guessed no, you would be correct.

The one-sided trial proceeded forward that day with a misled, carefully weeded, and hand-selected jury seated for a day of cleverly crafted lies and bogus claims presented by Mr. Petrocelli and his two coached witnesses.

The judge provided a set of instructions to the carefully weeded jury ordering them to accept without question a series of facts, none of which were true, and none of which ever had been adjudicated in a court of law. And guess who wrote the instructions.

At the conclusion of the trial, the judge signed without change (as usual), an order prepared by Lennar's lawyers that included a $100,000,000 mathematical error in Lennar's favor. Did he even bother to read it? And, in case it wasn't obvious enough that the judge was as far from impartial as it gets, he included this verbatim statement in his remarks as he wound up the trial:

"I Love Lennar."

And I am sure they loved him.

What transpired in the Miami courtroom on December 2, 2013 strikes at the heart of our judicial system. What was the devious path taken by Lennar and its lawyers to get to the courtroom after five years and tens of millions of dollars of shareholder money squandered in the process of asserting clearly meritless claims? Here is the answer to that question . . .

CHAPTER SEVENTEEN

Frivolous Claims and The Florida Fairy Tale

THE FLORIDA CASE was filed on behalf of Lennar by the same lawyer, Daniel Petrocelli, who unquestionably lied to jurors in a Miami courtroom. The filed claims are a Florida fairy tale.

The story is not unlike a Grimm's Fairy Tale — including a greedy king, a miller's daughter, and a malevolent elf who could spin straw into gold. For a steep price. And spin is the operative word in this case. How did they turn this straw into gold?

Petrocelli is clearly the malevolent elf. Stuart Miller plays two roles in this fairy tale, the greedy king and the miller's daughter. But that works, because he also plays multiple roles at Lennar.

Let's go back to July of 2008 and see just how Lennar and its lawyers were able to turn meritless claims into this insane verdict.

And if you are surprised at the wholesale subversion of our legal system and breathtaking dishonesty evidenced by the incontrovertible trial record presented in the preceding chapter, you haven't seen anything yet.

The long and tortuous journey in the Florida court started with a four page letter I wrote to the Lennar Board of Directors in July of 2008 expressing certain concerns. As outlined in a previous chapter, the letter was invited by the Lennar Board through a published and legally mandated process. And the allegations in the letter are as true today as they were when the letter was written.

Depositions of Lennar directors were taken and a key Lennar director, Irving Bolotin, testified in regard to his and the board's views as to whether or not it was proper to send such a letter to the board. It was. Lennar Director Irving Bolotin testified under oath on February 17, 2010. Here is what he said:

Q. Is it your view that the board of directors as a general matter has an interest in hearing about complaints that people may have about their dealings with Lennar?

A. Yes.

Q. And in fact, you welcome those complaints and have created specific mechanisms for making them; is that fair to say?

A. Yes, sir.

Q. Are people who have complaints about Lennar limited to using the hotline or are they permitted to otherwise communicate with the board?

A. It's a free country.

Q. You wouldn't view that as improper if somebody had a complaint about Lennar and rather use that hotline they use some other mechanism for communicating?

A. They're free to do so, and some people do that.

Q. Is it fair to say that you would welcome those types of com-munications as a mechanism for allowing people to air out whatever potential grievances they may have?

A. If anybody complains, we certainly would review those com-plaints.

Q. Is it fair to say that you would rather hear about the com-plaint that somebody has than not hear about it?

A. I would welcome hearing about it, yes. I can't speak for any-body else, but certainly I think — to properly operate your business from my perspective, it's a good idea to listen to those complaints that anybody may have.

Q. I want to ask you, sir, irrespective of the eventual conclusion that the board reached about this letter, are you glad that Mr. Marsch sent you his concerns in the form of a letter?

A. I think he had the right to send a letter, and I read it.

No Lennar director or representative of a director ever responded to the letter or contacted us or our counsel. And there is no evidence that any board member sug-gested that the proper response to the letter was a lawsuit.

Instead, the board members turned again to Mr. Petro-celli, asked his firm to investigate the allegations in the let-ter. And, no surprise, Petrocelli immediately advised Miller that Lennar should authorize him to prepare and file yet another expensive lawsuit in Florida within days of receipt of the letter.

This Florida lawsuit has cost Lennar shareholders tens of millions of dollars to date, has provided a windfall for at least four law firms employed by Lennar, and has been a showcase for an abuse of the legal process that is in a class by itself.

The filing of the Florida lawsuit accelerated the resource exhaustion process already underway in California. There were four distinct frauds-on-court contained in the Florida lawsuit.

Fraud Number One: The Board Letter. Lennar claimed that the letter to the Board was defamatory and extortion. It was neither. The letter was only sent to the Lennar Board, not the general public. Board members had no problem with it. And litigation was already pending with Lennar, complaints were filed, and they contained allegations far more extensive than that depicted in the letter. There is an applicable litigation privilege, and the letter could not have been defamatory. Nor could it be extortion. We were simply asking for money back improperly taken by Lennar.

It was just a letter sent by a frustrated partner to circumvent dishonest corporate management, communicate with the Board as I was invited to do, and try to get my money back. Jaffe's nonsense that "we lost money every year for 10 years" was just that: nonsense. And I was tired of it.

And, in fact, the Board letter was quite prescient in many ways. For example, here is just one passage from the letter:

> "Lennar, my fifty percent partner in HCC (and by extension the Bridges) has kept books and accounts for the Bridges project from the inception of HCC. None of Lennar's accounting

has added up from the very inception of the project, and despite numerous promises from Jon Jaffe, no useful accounting has ever been forthcoming with regard to HCC . . . Lennar's stated position, according to Jaffe, is that the Bridges development (and by extension HCC) has never been profitable."

The letter is exactly what Lennar purports to solicit regarding communications by interested parties to the Lennar board.

Fraud Number Two: Lennar amended their complaint to include allegations that the FDI Report was *"false and scurrilous"*, and caused huge damages to Lennar. There is ample proof that the FDI report was anything but *"false and scurrilous."* The truth may hurt, but telling it isn't actionable.

Fraud Number Three: False damages claims. In fact there were no damages to Lennar. A stock decline allegedly based on a truthful report isn't actionable in the first place, but it gets better: Lennar does not own its stock, the shareholders do. And no shareholder ever filed a lawsuit or asserted claims of any kind. All of Lennar's claims are meritless, and they know it. On top of that, Lennar never claimed one dollar of loss in any public filing including all of their mandated reports to the SEC. Ever.

Fraud Number Four. False evidence. Petrocelli and Lennar

manufactured claims that there were discovery violations that warranted suspending due process and used those claims to deprive the defendants of the right to contest Lennar's allegations. And Lennar and its lawyers employed the exact tactics used by plaintiffs' lawyers in the Chevron and Dole cases.

They used two fully compromised experts to mislead the court. A computer forensic expert and a damage expert. Lennar pawned off a supposed independent computer forensic expert who filed false and ghost-written reports with the court, and then used these fabricated reports to obtain unconscionable rulings. They then used these rulings to set up a one-sided trial to obtain a one billion dollar verdict. A verdict based on lies.

THE ROLE PLAYED by expert witnesses in the legal process can have a big impact. Just ask Chevron. Experts can be retained by either side in a legal dispute and, of course, that expert role is one of advocacy. Who would hire an expert that didn't agree with their position?

Another role played by expert witnesses in the legal process is that of a court-appointed expert witness. This role is fundamentally different from that of a plaintiffs' or defendants' expert. The duty of the court-appointed expert is to the court. And only to the court.

In January 2012, after they lost a major hearing in the Florida case, Lennar's lawyers put in motion an elaborate scheme to create evidentiary issues where none existed. Mr. Petrocelli jumped up in court after they lost and claimed that my computer hard drive had been wiped of critical data.

There is nothing new about Mr. Petrocelli and false evidentiary claims. This is the playbook he uses in many of his cases. First, fabricate claims regarding alleged mishandling of discovery issues and documents. Second, claim that the unavailability of key documents or alleged evidence (whether or not they exist or ever existed) impairs their ability to prosecute or defend their case or calculate damages. Then ask the court for an order precluding the other side from having the right to defend or prosecute the case. This makes it much easier to win especially when you didn't have a case in the first place. As was proven in Miami on December 2, 2013.

To put this scheme in motion, step one was to fabricate evidentiary issues, in this case, intentional computer wiping, and then seek appointment of an independent computer forensic expert to prove or disprove the wiping claim. And the court ordered the appointment of an independent computer forensics expert to assess Mr. Petrocelli's' claims. We welcomed this process because we knew the claims were just made up and that a true independent computer forensics professional would quickly debunk these falsified and baseless claims.

But in this case, for Lennar, only one independent expert would do among the thousands of qualified experts in the field of computer forensics. His name is Scott Cooper, a principal in a the firm of Pegasus Squire Inc. located on Wilshire Blvd. in Los Angeles, CA, not far from Petrocelli's office. And Lennar's lawyers fought for months to get him, and only him, appointed as the purported court-appointed expert.

But they apparently forgot to mention to Mr. Cooper he was a court-appointed independent expert, with duties to the court and only the court.

Cooper testified under oath that he didn't know he was an independent court-appointed expert, or a court-appointed expert at all. And then produced a declaration signed by him under penalty of perjury stating:

"Pegasus (Cooper) was retained by O'Melveny & Myers LLP (OMM) in this matter as electronic discovery and litigation consultants on behalf of their client, Lennar Corp. I declare under penalty of perjury . . . the forgoing is true and correct."

Guess what: he could not possibly have been a "discovery and litigation consultant" to Lennar, and at the same time be a true independent court-appointed expert.

But it gets worse: while testifying on the matter in court Cooper further announced that he was refusing to turn over key information to our lawyers, including all of his communications with the Lennar lawyers, citing privilege between him and his law firm: O'Melveny & Myers. He was also a client of O'Melveny & Myers, a fact he had conveniently forgotten to mention until it was elicited in cross examination on the witness stand.

What was Lennar and its lawyers hiding behind this absurd claim of privilege? In fact, how could an attorney-client privilege be asserted between plaintiff's lawyers and a supposed independent court-appointed expert? And, worse, used to hide communications between the supposed independent expert and Lennar's lawyers. Why didn't the judge halt the proceedings after that revelation and order that a true independent expert instead of the obviously fully-compromised charlatan sitting in front of him?

Cooper further admitted that he worked both out of Mr. Petrocelli's offices in Los Angeles, and in Lennar's lawyers' office in Miami.

It was clear that Cooper was clearly in the role of advocate, and just as clear that he was not an independent court-appointed expert. This is not what the court ordered.

The plan was to foist off Mr. Cooper on the court in Miami as an independent court-appointed computer forensic expert, then influence, direct, and even ghost-write his reports. Then use those reports to set the table for a series of punitive orders. This scheme was successful, and those orders led inexorably to the one-sided trial that occurred on December 2, 2013.

So, much as in the Chevron case, although Mr. Cooper could not meet a single test of the independence required of a court-appointed computer expert, this thoroughly compromised expert and his ghost-written reports and rehearsed testimony were ultimately the keys to obtaining a billion dollar judgment.

In the Chevron case, as reported in Mr. Barrett's book, *Law of the Jungle,* Mr. Donziger, the plaintiff's lawyer who sued Chevron, was quoted as saying "Facts do not exist. Facts are created." This is certainly the model followed by Lennar's lawyers and their experts.

The forensics task ordered by the court was primarily to prove or disprove Mr. Petrocelli's baseless accusation of computer wiping. This is a simple job for a qualified forensics professional, and, as is often the case in this story, another binary issue arises: either the accusation of wiping was true or it was false.

Any competent computer forensic professional could do this job and, at most, the cost would be a few thousand dollars, and the time frame would be no more than a few weeks.

When Mr. Petrocelli's machinations finally led to Mr. Cooper and only Mr. Cooper's involvement in the forensic process, we, to be on the safe side, located and retained a top-of-the-profession computer forensic expert, Mr. John Jorgensen of Florida-based Sylint Corp. to perform the same simple task assigned to Mr. Cooper.

Mr. Jorgensen's client list includes but is not limited to the FBI, the NSA, the Department of Defense, the governments of Egypt, Kuwait, Malaysia, England, South Korea, and Germany. He is at the top of his profession. And he worked directly at the NSA for a number of years doing highly classified sophisticated computer forensic analysis. He and his firm could definitely handle an analysis of a $700.00 basic single hard drive desktop computer.

Mr. Cooper, Lennar's expert, began a forensic analysis of the computer in question and began turning out a series of reports, each one more ridiculous than the last. This went on for months. For a task that any competent professional would view as a one or two week job. And the reports alleged wholesale wiping just like Mr. Petrocelli's breathless accusations to the court.

What an amazing coincidence! The reports ended up mirroring Petrocelli's unfounded accusations, even though Petrocelli never had access to my computer and would not have had any idea what may or may not be in it.

And not surprisingly, the reports looked a lot like they were ghost written by Mr. Petrocelli and his Enron team, and were obviously reverse-engineered to fit Petrocelli's accusations.

It was crucial to Petrocelli's strategy to have such reports in hand in order to execute his standard play: fabricate an evidentiary issue and then trump it up into sanctions and a default. Divert the court's attention from the actual case at hand. Thus he avoids having to try a meritless case and avoids putting his clients on the stand in front of a jury to be exposed as the liars they are. Straw into gold.

And as the ever more lurid reports continued to flow from Mr. Cooper, something else was flowing as well. Money was changing hands, a lot of it, from Lennar to Mr. Cooper. Almost $1,000,000 for a $5,000 job. That is bribery, and it is simply above the table, instead of below.

Mr. Jorgensen, our forensic computer expert, also created a report and submitted it to the court. Not surprisingly, his forensic report was the polar opposite of Mr. Cooper's, and categorically stated that there was nothing whatsoever out of the ordinary with my computer, no wiping, and that there was no basis at all for the findings in Mr. Coopers' reports.

And in a cross examination of Mr. Jorgensen in the

Miami courtroom, neither Lennar's lawyers nor even the judge, Jose Rodriguez, could refute one word of Mr. Jorgenson's report, or his testimony. Not one.

Nonetheless, despite overwhelming evidence to the contrary, the judge again signed, unchanged, yet another Where-Do-I-Sign order written by Mr. Petrocelli and his co-counsel Mr. Gersten.

This punitive order contained numerous falsehoods, fabricated facts and even ascribed conduct that was literally impossible according to one of the most qualified forensic analyst firms in the business. But now the deck was stacked, the cards were marked, and the game commenced.

One amusing side note in this process was that Mr. Cooper spent a great deal of time in testimony explaining how smart he was in general, and how experienced he was in computer forensics. He even claimed to be a member of Mensa. Then he went on to testify that my computer was selectively wiped by techniques so sophisticated that even he couldn't figure it out.

But there was no evidence offered that I had either any specialized computer knowledge or ever hired anyone who did. The only way I could wipe a computer would be with a soft cloth.

So the predictable trial result was the end game of one of the largest frauds ever perpetrated in a United States court room by a plaintiff and its lawyers.

The trial was over, and now it was media spin time. Minutes after obtaining the "hard fought" verdict, Petrocelli sprinted to the phones to call his favorite reporters and report the results of the jury trial and the billion dollar result. His biggest legal victory ever! What an impressive lawyer! A career high! And with another certifiable Shining Star and Wonderful Company for a client!

Apparently he neglected to mention to the press that it was a one-sided trial, the deck was stacked, the judge was co-opted, the jury was carefully selected from the remaining candidates who had not voiced due process concerns, that he and a Lennar executive had lied repeatedly to the jurors, and that their phony damage expert could barely balance a checkbook.

Stuart Miller wasted no time producing a press release that said:

"... *The true value of the verdict is the validation of our integrity, credibility and transparency, which have always been cornerstones of our foundation.*"

And he went on to say:

"*The jury award represents a complete vindication of Lennar's reputation and good name.*"

Oh really? By having Lennar fund and actively participate in one of the biggest fraud-on-the-court cases in the history of the country? And Miller himself sat by and cheered Petrocelli on as he overtly compromised the cornerstone and the foundation of our legal system: due process, impartial judges, the jury system, the right to counsel, trial on the merits, the right to present evidence, and the right to face your accusers.

Integrity? Not by a long shot, unless the word has been redefined recently to include fraud, fraud in the inducement, fraudulent transfers, conversion, extortion, undermining the court system, lying in court, lying to U.S. Attorneys, bankruptcy fraud, and stealing from partners.

Credibility? Take their word at your peril. Lennars' executives and their lawyers are proven liars.

Transparency? We couldn't get accounting from them for hundreds of millions of dollars no matter what we tried. You can't see into the Black Box no matter how close you get.

It goes without saying, but let's say it anyway: Lennar's lawyers and executives lied to prospective jurors and empanelled jurors in Miami, and Lennar executives attended, listened to, condoned, and supported that conduct. Is there any doubt that this conduct has been representative of their behavior since Stuart Miller took control of the company? Wholesale looting and pervasive lying were the order of the day.

And what must have transpired in their three hundred or so other off-balance ventures could have been as bad or worse. Look at Jaffe's treatment of RFC at the same time and in the same deal as the Miller/Seikely double-date bailout at shareholder expense.

And it was a good thing for Lennar that they could arrange this ludicrous trial process in hometown Miami. If there had been a real trial, Stuart Miller, instead of sitting in the front row for the shareholder-funded show with a smirk on his face, would have had to testify. And eat every single one of his and his lawyers' false statements, and own up to the factual basis for each and every one of the FDI Red Flags. Plus the revelations included in the whistle-blower letter and the falsity of the non-existent damage claims.

Lennar CFO Bruce Gross would have been torn to shreds trying to pawn off on a jury his nonsense about Lennar's integrity and fairness. His coached, rehearsed, and utterly concocted story regarding the Lakes was ludicrous.

And their damage expert was a piece of work. In the opening minutes of a deposition he was caught submitting a false resume. It turned out that he was unable to pass even a basic Chartered Financial Analyst exam after two tries and had given up. So Lennar had an "expert" testifying as to hundreds of millions in alleged damages who couldn't even pass an exam that many thousands in the country routinely take and pass as they pursue their careers.

As noted in the *Law of the Jungle,* the judge in Chevron v. Donziger included the following statement in a 485 page ruling on the case:

"If ever there were a case warranting equitable relief with respect to a judgment procured by fraud, this is it."

And certainly the same sentiment applies here.

This fraud-on-the-court verdict obtained in Miami is now on appeal, and it will be informative to see what the 3rd District Court of Appeals in Miami thinks about cooked-up damage claims, rigged experts, Where-Do-I-Sign court orders, denial of counsel, suspension of constitutional rights and due process, wholesale lying to jurors by Lennar's lawyers and executives, and the not-so-impartial "I-Love-Lennar" judge. A trial without the ability for both sides to present and contest evidence isn't a trial, it is a farce. And there is a right to counsel. Maybe Miller will get his chance on the stand at some point in time, if we can keep their thumbs off of the scales of justice.

CHAPTER EIGHTEEN

A Liar for Hire

"The entire judicial system relies on the integrity of its proceedings and the lawyers' duty of candor with the court."
Quote taken from *Tangled Webs* by James B. Stewart

A LAW LICENSE may be a license to steal, but it isn't a license to lie. Daniel Petrocelli is a one-man excavation crew who has made a career out of undermining the foundation of our U.S. justice system.

The role played by Petrocelli and his Enron team in this story can't be overstated. Lennar knew how to steal, but they needed professional help to manipulate and exploit the legal system in order to keep their ill-gotten gains.

The trial that took place in Miami was the pinnacle of his career. A billion dollar verdict! What a lawyer!

But an examination of just how that verdict was obtained reveals that his entire vile and detestable skill set was required to pull it off. His skill set included lying to jurors. Obtaining punitive court orders by submitting doctored expert reports to the court. Suborning perjury from coached witnesses. Collaborating with a judge to mislead, inflame, and outright lie to an unsuspecting jury. Undermining due process and constitutional rights. And all while operating as an officer of the court.

And in reality, the case brought by him in Miami on behalf of Lennar was so defective that the only way he could possibly succeed would have been to set up a one-sided trial. A trial on the merits would have quickly revealed that . . . there was no merit to the claims. Yet the absurdity of the proceedings, as pointed out by certain prospective jurors, compelled him to lie to a jury anyway just to ensure a win. This despicable conduct is the measure of the man.

Could anybody reading this story seriously conclude anything other than that any lawyer that would tell calculated lies to a jury and co-opt the court process in Miami would also habitually lie in other court proceedings, co-opt other judges, arrange and submit false expert reports in other cases, and undermine the legal system from coast to coast in every conceivable venue?

With his client and co-conspirator Stuart Miller in tow, he brazenly walked into the U.S. Attorney's office in Miami, lied to not one but two U.S. Attorneys and presented falsified evidence alleging criminal conduct. All in effort to gain an advantage in a civil dispute. Anything to win.

Comparing him to a virus would be unfair — to a virus. He infects every proceeding and everyone with whom he comes in contact. There is no more skilled liar in the country.

He may even be a pathological liar. The basic traits of a pathological liar include lying frequently, lying habitually, and lying compulsively. He knew there was a court reporter in the courtroom on December 2, 2013. And he had already compromised the proceeding to ensure a win. But he could not help himself: he still lied on the record to a jury, regardless of the consequences.

Pathological liars create and live in a fantasy world. This trait ties perfectly with the alternate universe he creates for clients as outlined in this book.

He is a perfect fit for today's corporate criminal: they are greedy, have no scruples, and will stop at nothing. He is the same, if not worse. It takes a thoroughly dishonest lawyer to abandon principles and actively seek to undermine our country's all-important legal system from the inside. Anything to win, and all just for money and self-aggrandizement.

He lies with impunity and at apparently no risk of getting caught. How many other wrongful verdicts have been obtained for other corporate clients with the use of his unique skill set? How many other reputations have been destroyed with the use of his character assassination and smear tactics? It certainly wasn't just chance that Lennar hired him and the entire Skilling/Enron defense team.

CHAPTER NINETEEN

RICO: The Lennar Way

IN 1970 CONGRESS passed the Organized Crime Control Act that included the Racketeer Influenced and Corruption Organizations Act or RICO.

Racketeering is defined as obtaining or extorting money illegally or carrying on illegal business activities. A pattern of illegal activity carried out as part of an enterprise that is owned or controlled by those who are engaged in the illegal activity constitutes racketeering. A pattern consists of "at least two acts of racketeering activity."

There is a long list of illegal acts that qualify under these statutes, and here is a representative but not comprehensive list:

- Bribery
- Embezzlement from Pension and Welfare Funds
- Mail Fraud
- Wire Fraud
- Financial Institution Fraud
- Obstruction of Justice

- Obstruction of Criminal Investigation
- Witness Tampering
- Retaliation Against Witness
- Extortion
- Money Laundering
- Bankruptcy Fraud
- Violation of the Currency and Foreign Transactions Reporting Act
- Fraud in Connection With Access Devices.

RICO penalties are severe and include exposure to treble damages. Any two or more of the above acts within a ten year period qualify as a pattern under RICO.

It is as if Lennar executives and their lawyers used the above list as a checklist to make sure they didn't miss any counts. Few, if any, companies and individuals in this country cry out louder for prosecution, fines, restitution, and jail terms. Let's look at a sample list of Lennar and its executives' conduct over the last several years to see how overqualified they are under RICO statutes:

LandSource/CALPERS/Barclays Bank: Much has been written about this fraudulent transaction elsewhere in this book, but suffice it to say that Lennar and its executives qualify under at least three RICO counts on this one:

- Financial Institution Fraud
- Fraud in the Inducement
- Fraudulent Transfer

FDIC Ft. Myers Claim: The FDIC fraud claim against

Lennar Corporation in Ft. Myers Florida has also been examined elsewhere in this book, but Lennar's use of false
appraisals and fake straw buyers to defraud a financial institution out of millions of dollars certainly fits squarely
within any reasonable RICO analysis. It is a pattern of conduct. And, early in 2014, a Federal district judge summarily denied Lennar's motion to dismiss the FDIC's
complaint, citing that the complaint against Lennar Corp
more than met the requirements for a claim of fraud
and/or negligent inducement. Lennar and its executives
qualify under at least two counts on this one:

- Financial Institution Fraud
- Fraud in the Inducement

Miami Criminal Complaint: Lennar, its executives, and
its lawyers made false statements and sent letters containing
false and misleading statements to the U.S. Attorney's office
In Miami, Florida. This subject is covered in detail in a preceding chapter, but to summarize, they first engaged in a resource exhaustion process, squandered millions of shareholder
dollars, carefully ascertained that the target was financially exhausted, and then made false statements to a U.S. Attorney to
obtain a false plea under duress and under the threat of a
lengthy jail sentence. Daniel Petrocelli and Stuart Miller personally engaged in this process and conspired to make false
statements to not one, but two U. S. Attorneys.

They then used this false plea to obtain an advantage in
civil proceedings in other venues, including a bankruptcy
proceeding. This is a crime. Lennar, its executives, and its

attorneys qualify on at least three counts on this one:

- Lying to a U.S. Attorney
- Obstruction of Justice
- Bankruptcy Fraud
- Conspiracy

Miami Lawsuit: In Florida, in a lawsuit directed at my company and me, Lennar and its lawyers foisted off a close associate and client of Lennar's law firm as a purported court-appointed independent expert witness. This subject is covered in a preceding chapter. They obtained a verdict in excess of one billion dollars by engaging in a systematic fraud on the court. Lennar, its executives, and its lawyers qualify on at least two counts on this one:

- Obstruction of Justice
- Witness Tampering

Contractor Extortion: In the first quarter of 2007 headlines in numerous publications, including the *San Diego Union Tribune, Contractor Magazine*, and other publications in Lennar home-building market areas told the same story: Lennar was strong-arming and extorting its contractors and subcontractors — for example, this from *PRNewswire* February 27, 2007:

National Builder Reneges On Contracts, Threatens Trades.

The article reports that various trade contractors working on building projects with Lennar Corporation had received letters from the builder directing subcontractors to reduce and resubmit invoices for previously contracted work. Within the letters, Lennar threatened the contractors with being shut out of future work unless they meet the company's demand to lower prices for work in progress, and in many cases, work already completed. The penalty for non-compliance with their demands was not only to be excluded from future work, but it was also clear that Lennar had no intention of paying for the already-performed fraudulently-induced work until if and when the subcontractor/victim "agreed" to the reduced payment.

The California Professional Association of Specialty Contractors (CALPASC) correctly called this extortion and referred the matter to the California Attorney General and local district attorneys for review. Similar conduct took place in other states and the conduct also was referred to District Attorneys in a number of states.

Certainly this conduct could be viewed, in addition to extortion, as one of Lennar's favorite tactics: fraud in the inducement. How many contractors and subcontractors would have proceeded with work if they had known Lennar's true intentions? This is just another example of Lennar's typical hidden agenda at work.

The fact that Lennar signed agreements with contractors and subcontractors, let them in many cases complete their side of the bargain, and then demanded a large discount proves a number of things about Lennar: written agreements mean nothing to them. That is my experience. There is a hidden agenda in place at all times. That is also my experience. Extorting thinly-capitalized subcontractors is all in a day's work for them. It's the Lennar Way.

Another cavalier and manipulative use of Lennar's contractors, subcontractors, and suppliers was the cynical and secretly planned bankruptcy of LandSource. Lennar and the Lennar executives qualify on at least two counts on this one:

- Extortion
- Fraud in the Inducement

Bankruptcy Fraud and Extortion: The bankruptcy court is an Alice-In-Wonderland environment where everything is inside out and upside down. It was actually beneficial to Lennar to have a large group of unsecured creditors in the LandSource bankruptcy process. They became a separate voting class that could be extorted and manipulated in the process. And that is exactly what happened. So Lennar signed many, many contracts for work knowing they had no intention of paying.

I am not speculating or guessing on this. I served on the LandSource unsecured creditors committee and observed first-hand the anguish caused by the cynical manipulation of these victims. Here is how it worked: Lennar contracted to spend hundreds of millions of dollars for services, supplies, and construction contracts, knowing a bankruptcy filing for LandSource was inevitable. And there were over 5,000 similarly situated unsecured creditors.

Then came the payment of the special dividend to Lennar and its sister company LNR. The special dividend was a fraudulent transfer and left LandSource technically insolvent and unable to pay its bills. The complaint filed by the unsecured creditors in the LandSource bankruptcy got it right, stating:

Plaintiff is informed and believes and thereon asserts that the Fraudulent Transfer left Debtors with inadequate cash for operating expenses and to service its debt, as evidenced by Debtors' financial condition following the Fraudulent Transfer.

Lennar knew that there would not be adequate funds to both service the massive interest payments due in connection with the special dividend and also pay contractual payments as they became due in the normal course of business. Lennar also knew there was a bankruptcy filing inevitably coming and they needed an unsecured class of creditors as part of that process. As Stuart Miller testified: *". . . we try to do things strategically and by plan."*

And an additional benefit of the cynical use of these unsuspecting contractors, subcontractors, and suppliers was that at the end of the bankruptcy process, the unsecured creditors would be forced to take huge writedowns and LandSource, still controlled by Lennar, would retain the benefit of their work and services.

I spoke with a number of contractors who were extorted by Lennar executives. They recounted stories about threatening phone calls to their homes at night by Lennar executives to demand acceptance of Lennar's punitive bankruptcy plan as a condition for future work. Sound familiar? — The exact same thuggish, extortive, and illegal tactics they employed against subcontractors across the country in the first quarter of 2007. This is a pattern.

We reviewed a number of representative complaints filed across the country that prove a pattern of conduct by Lennar that can only be categorized as racketeering. Their criminal conduct is amazingly similar in so many cases. Lennar and the Lennar executives qualify on this one on at least three counts:

- Fraud in the Inducement
- Bankruptcy Fraud
- Fraudulent Transfer

Florida Land Fraud: Here is a perfect example: two companion cases filed in 2009 in Osceola County, Florida provide a detailed example of a signature Lennar fraud.

Lennar was sued for the following counts: fraudulent misrepresentation, breach of fiduciary duty, breach of contract, tortious interference with an advantageous business relationship, usurpation of a corporate opportunity, and breach of implied covenant of good faith and fair dealing.

Any of this sound familiar? This complaint reads like it was taken word for word from the Lakes complaint appellate ruling quoted in Chapter 15 of this book on the Lakes development project Lennar hijacked from our Bridges development company.

Here are the essential details of this appalling story of fraud and deception. The story begins in 2004 with a local developer in Osceola County, Florida that had plans to subdivide their land and build 626 residential homesites. As the planning process got underway, Lennar Corp entered the picture and proposed to buy the planned homesites when completed and on an agreed schedule and at agreed prices. Simple, right? Nope. Nothing is ever as it seems with Lennar.

An agreement was reached between the development company and U.S. Home/Lennar (They are one and the same and will be referred to as Lennar). Planning and permitting continued for the project through 2005. In 2006, with a signed agreement with Lennar in hand, the developers approached a local bank to arrange infrastructure construction financing for homesites, utilities, roads, guard gates, and a clubhouse. This financing was readily accomplished and infrastructure construction proceeded.

In late 2007, the developers delivered the first 48 homesites to Lennar as per the signed agreement. Lennar refused to pay or take delivery of these homesites, citing that *"Lennar's corporate philosophy had changed"* and that they had no intention of honoring their contractual obligations to buy finished homesites.

But as always, Lennar had it all planned out in advance:

• Lennar had maneuvered itself into a position where they could indefinitely tie up the development company's property even though Lennar was not honoring the contractual terms of the agreement.

• Lennar through its actions could and did cause a default in the construction loan agreement thus causing distress for both the lender and the development company.

• Lennar then secretly met with the now distressed project lender and purchased the construction loan and mortgage at a steep discount.

• Lennar then commenced a foreclosure on the now-developed property to force out their "partners", and usurp the opportunity for themselves.

And if there is some notion that it was low or mid-level Lennar executives committing these crimes, here is a direct quote from the operative complaint:

Lennar president Stuart Miller toured the project unannounced . . . and said Lennar was "behind the project 140%." This was, of course, a lie, and in reality Lennar failed to take down any homesites on the agreed terms at the agreed prices, and was waiting to complete the secret deal with the construction lender, foreclose the loan, and usurp the opportunity for itself.

And having Stuart Miller "behind you" sounds like the makings of a Greek tragedy.

Lennar and its executives qualify on at least three counts on this one:

• Fraud
• Fraud in the Inducement
• Financial Institution Fraud

Phone Hacking: We have convincing circumstantial evidence that Lennar and its lawyers engaged in illegal surveillance and phone hacking involving my company and me. On January 9, 2012, a highly sophisticated hacking team began the process of hacking my phone. This hacking team was operating simultaneously in at least two states, California and Louisiana. In the initial phase of the process, they obtained the necessary information to access my phone by impersonating me to my cell phone carrier, AT&T.

On January 11, 2012 I had made plans to travel to Florida to attend yet another hearing in Lennar's frivolous lawsuit filed in Miami. And Lennar's lawyers were aware of my travel plans.

In the afternoon of January 11, at 2:02 pm, at a time when I was supposed to be on a lengthy flight to Miami from San Diego, the hackers called AT&T, impersonated me, had vital personal information, claimed "I" had lost my SIM card, and a new one was issued immediately. Now the hackers had unrestricted access to my phone and all the data it contained.

This data included phone books, phone call records, email, and text messages. And this data included privileged communications and numerous unlisted and otherwise inaccessible phone numbers.

Not long after the phone hack, pretext calls were made to certain unlisted numbers in the hacked phone in order to obtain information about me. Information that Lennar had been seeking unsuccessfully in other forums. And it is a fact that the hack occurred when I had planned to travel to Florida, but my plans changed at the last minute, and the trip was delayed for two days.

My phone suddenly went dead when the hack occurred because the SIM had been transferred. I, of course, did not realize that the phone had been hacked, and just assumed it was a carrier problem. Accordingly, I went to a local AT&T store, reported the problem, a new SIM was installed, and the phone worked again.

It wasn't until reports surfaced about the pretext calls that I deduced that the phone had been hacked. Meanwhile, the hackers had obtained personal and private communications and other data.

And I believed and still believe that it was Lennar and its lawyers who ordered this hack, and obtained the data. What are the chances that a pretext caller or callers would have the names and unlisted phone numbers out of my phone and be calling within days to seek the exact information that Lennar was seeking in other venues?

I hired the top telephone hacking forensic analyst in the country, Ben Levitan, to investigate the phone hack and prepare a report. Here are some quotes from his executive summary:

> *"It is my opinion that the victim, Mr. Nicolas Marsch's phone was hijacked for the purpose of obtaining private communications between Mr. Marsch and other parties that were stored in his phone . . . "*
>
> *"The perpetrators had then successfully taken control of Mr. Marsch's phone and were able to access all of his private communications stored in the AT & T network."*
>
> *"I further conclude that Mr. Marsch's phone service was intentionally hijacked, and he was the specific*

target of the perpetrators."

In a deposition taken on August 13, 2012, our counsel questioned Jon Jaffe extensively on the subject of phone hacking and surveillance of me by Lennar and Lennar's lawyers. He was instructed nine times not to answer by Lennar's lawyers and cited "attorney-client privilege and work product" as the reason for the instruction not answer. Think about that instruction for a minute. It sounded a lot like pleading the Fifth Amendment. Lennar and its executives qualify on at least one count on this one:

• Wire Fraud

These representative examples of Lennar's RICO — qualified behavior compare with many other similar situations involving Lennar across the country. For example, after comparing the LandSource fraud and the FDIC complaint one can only conclude that each of these carefully thought out and well-executed frauds are business as usual for Lennar. What you see in this book is the tip of the iceberg. And there are many more victims out there with similar stories.

Despite all the name calling, finger pointing, character assassination, lying, and false accusations directed toward me and my company, the reality is that it is only Lennar that is a defendant in many, many fraud lawsuits across the country, and who has engaged in up to ten of the explicit acts listed as RICO violations.

They have a pattern and practice of deceptive behavior.

The old saying "Where there is smoke there is fire" isn't descriptive enough for this situation. This is more like a raging inferno of fraud, theft, and deceit on a national scale.

Researching and detailing all of the Lennar fraudulent acts across the country would be a book in itself. And that may be our next project. As the whistleblower wrote:

"As a manager, I have witnessed endless improprieties made by Stuart Miller, Jon Jaffe, and management."

The deeper you dig, the more you find on this financial crime in progress also known as Lennar.

OTHERS GET PUNISHED for behavior that isn't nearly as calculated and fraudulent as Lennar's everyday conduct. Several multi-billion dollar settlements have been reached recently with banks and others by U.S. authorities related to mortgage fraud. Specifically the charges were that the institutions had packaged substandard mortgages and sold them to unwary buyers. The essence of the charges was the deliberate withholding of key information to fraudulently induce others to buy packages of substandard or non-performing mortgages. For example, Citigroup just settled such a claim on July 14, 2014 for a total of $7,000,000,000. Four billion of that settlement will go to the Justice Department for a civil penalty, and five hundred million will go to the FDIC. (and the FDIC will need it if they keep doing business with Lennar). The balance goes to states and consumer relief.

What is the difference between that and Lennar submitting inflated appraisals and falsified cash flows to fraudulently obtain $1,400,000,000, or submitting inflated appraisals and straw buyers to defraud a predecessor institution to the FDIC.

And what is the difference between the illegal use of insider information for gain and Lennar withholding key information from CALPERS and Barclays Bank to induce the bank to loan $1,400,000,000?

Insider trading convictions make the news on a regular basis today. Huge fines and jail terms are the order of the day in a vast majority of these cases. The prosecutors in the Southern District of New York have an incredible win streak going, with a 99% conviction rate in cases brought by them.

And the purported losses or illicit gains from typical insider trading activities range from tens of millions to, in some cases, hundreds of millions of dollars or more. But they rarely get into the billion dollar range. A successfully prosecuted case can often turn on one email. Here, there is a truckload of evidence that Lennar withheld key information and committed loan fraud in the process.

And, in terms of alleged criminal acts and sentencing, size matters. In September 2014 Mathew Martoma was sentenced to nine years for his participation in an insider trading scheme. The sentence was directly relevant to the alleged dollar gain attributed to the scheme: $275,000,000.

They lied to me to gain access to hundreds of millions of dollars in cash. They fraudulently obtained

$1,400,000,000 by lying to pensioners and investors. The stakes here are higher by far than even the typical insider trading case.

SHERRON WATKINS, THE Enron whistleblower, in an interview with the *Guardian* on June 21, 2003, put it best. She said: "I don't think Enron is that unusual. After all, we have a chief executive class which act like dictators of small Latin American countries." Sounds a lot like Stuart Miller. In Miami.

And she went on to say in the same interview in regard to the Sarbanes Oxley Act of 2002 which require CEOs and CFOs to certify that financial statements are true and accurate under threat of up to 20 years in prison: "*Monetary fines don't do it. If you've made a hundred million dollars and you are fined $25,000,000, you're still filthy rich. To go to jail scares these guys to death. Standing in a cafeteria line for food, communal showers? It will change them forever.*"

The Lennar Way of doing business coast to coast has left a serial killer's trail of financial victims. Dishonored contracts, unpaid loans, contractors cheated, bills unpaid, looted companies, lies to U.S. Attorneys, pension funds hijacked, venture partners cheated, judges co-opted. Why should this behavior continue to go unpunished?

Let's list their identifiable Rico-Eligible counts so far:

• Fraud
• Financial Institution Fraud
• Fraud in the Inducement

- Fraudulent Transfer
- Bankruptcy Fraud
- Obstruction of Justice
- Witness Tampering
- Lying to a U.S. Attorney
- Extortion
- Wire Fraud
- Conspiracy

In a perfect world, corporate and personal fines and restitution are the minimum penalty that Lennar and its executives should be facing for this national crime spree. The minimum. But anyone who reads a newspaper once in a while knows that it most definitely isn't a perfect world.

It may be that the Lennar executives and their lawyers really are above the law and have get-out-of-jail free cards in their pockets. Who knows?

My experience with them indicates that it will take the resources and power of the government to bring these criminals to justice. Who else has the resources, the capability, and the responsibility?

Lennar thought nothing of spending over $100,000,000 in corporate resources just to try to silence and destroy a single venture partner who had the temerity to ask for an accounting for hundreds of millions of dollars flowing through (and out the back door) of an equally-owned company.

An examination of case after case across the country reveals a pattern of behavior that more than qualifies them for prosecution under the RICO statutes and most probably under U.S. Code Section 848—Continuing Criminal Enterprise also referred to as "CCE."

CHAPTER TWENTY

Just the Facts

IN 1995, WHEN I invited Lennar to participate with me as co-developer of the now world-famous Bridges golf course and residential development, I could not possibly have foreseen this outcome. From my side, every promise was kept, every term was honored, and every projected financial metric was exceeded.

I did my homework on them, but could not have possibly anticipated the transformation of Lennar from a straightforward homebuilder to the company it is today.

It was disconcerting to find myself in business with a company that suddenly began generating headlines like this:

Sacramento Bee — **Calpers Defrauded in $922 Million LandSource Deal**

Zero Hedge — **Calpers in Dire Straits Following Huge Investment Losses, Asks for $600 Million In Funding from**

Bankrupt California

SF Public Press — **Home-builder Lennar Uses Federal Taxpayer to Balance its Books**

Fraud Files — **Lennar CEO Lies About losses in Joint Venture**

PRNews Wire — **National Builder Reneges on Contracts, Threatens Trades**

Ft. Myers News-Press — **Chinese Drywall Fears Widen in SW Florida**

Ft. Myers News-Press — **Lennar accused of Fraud**

SD Union Tribune — **Former CCDC President Testifies to Ethics Panel**

What other company comes to mind that is routinely associated with headlines like these?

Lennar has been referred to in this book as a crime in progress and that is truer today than ever before. They are toxic, and everything they touch takes on a noxious odor.

For example, in California they have been caught numerous times improperly influencing elected or appointed officials, but are never penalized.

In fact, Lennar's consultant on at least two major redevelopment projects in San Francisco, Keith Jackson, was indicted in April of 2014 on charges, including racketeering and murder for hire. A perfect fit.

In San Diego, Nancy Graham, the former head of the non-profit Center City Development Corporation, a very important agency in charge of re-development of downtown San Diego, was forced to step down. It was revealed that she had received millions of dollars from Lennar Corporation while negotiating a lucrative hotel deal on behalf of the City of San Diego with them but failed to disclose this fact on conflict-of-interest forms she signed under penalty of perjury. And, to be sure, Lennar also failed to mention this fact during the negotiation process.

A reasoned and informed analysis of their conduct gleaned from the Lennar executives' own testimony, their actions, court records, court transcripts, documents, and news sources yield a series of incontrovertible facts. Here are ten of them.

Fact #1: In a Miami courtroom on December 2, 2013 Lennar's lawyers and a cooperative trial judge misled and lied to jurors in a one-sided trial and falsely obtained a one billion dollar verdict.

And Lennar's chief financial officer, Bruce Gross, appeared as a witness and also lied to the jury. It is impossible to reconcile his trial testimony with the well-documented facts presented in Chapter 15 of this book on the Lakes transaction. This trial followed a series of punitive and unsupportable rulings submitted by Lennar's lawyers and signed without change by the Miami trial judge and his predecessor.

Lennar and its lawyers have been subverting, undermining, and abusing the legal system from the day I filed claims to try and recover hundreds of millions of dollars in cash and other assets improperly taken from our jointly-owned development company.

Fact #2: Lennar used inflated appraisals and fraudulent cash flow projections to swindle CALPERS and Barclays Bank out of well over one billion dollars. And in the process also cheated over 5,000 unsecured creditors of LandSource LLC.

Fact #3: Lennar used inflated appraisals (again) and straw buyers to defraud the FDIC in Ft. Myers, Florida.

Fact #4: Lennar looted our jointly-owned Bridges development company. At the direction of Stuart Miller and Jon Jaffe, they misappropriated a profitable development opportunity belonging to our jointly-owned Bridges company and secretly conveyed it to one of Mr. Miller's personal friends. As the real estate market turned, Stuart Miller then directed Lennar to buy out his friends' multiple real estate positions at a profit thereby insuring a large loss to Lennar shareholders.

Fact #5: The FDI Ten Red Flags were generally accurate, even prescient at times, were not *false and scurrilous* as Lennar claimed, were not actionable, and were not a legitimate basis for a complaint to the U.S. Attorneys' office or a lawsuit in Miami.

Fact #6: Stuart Miller actively supported and directed

Lennar to fund a lawsuit in Florida falsely claiming damages in connection with a letter to the board of directors, the publication of the FDI report, and falsely-claimed damages in connection with a bailout of one of Miller's personal friends.

Fact #7: Stuart Miller, as CEO of Lennar, never signed a single 10K or 10Q report under penalty of perjury to the SEC that contained or reported "losses" attributable to the letter to the board, the FDI Red Flags publication, or to his personally-arranged bailout of his friends at Lennar shareholder expense.

Fact #8: Stuart Miller and Daniel Petrocelli conspired and lied to U.S. Attorneys in Miami about alleged damages to Lennar tied to publication of the FDI report and orchestrated a false plea obtained under duress.

Fact #9: Lennar and its lawyers then used this false under-duress plea to mislead courts in California and Florida and illegally obtain tens of millions of dollars in cash, valuable assets, and egregious rulings in favor of Lennar.

Fact #10: Lennar has concealed the identity and contact information of the author of a whistleblower letter written to me. Three top Lennar executives, Stuart Miller, Jon Jaffe, and Mark Sustana provided three completely different stories at the same time on that topic in under-oath testimony. They lied.

IN A TWIST on yet another notable whistleblower's advice, offered in the Watergate investigation, the best way to analyze a typical Lennar fraud is to: "follow the money." Disregard whatever misleading explanations or diversions they and their lawyers come up with, and instead simply note that no matter whose money it is to start with, the money always ends up in Lennar's pocket.

It is another absolute fact that those at the top influence the culture of any organization. For good or for evil. Look at Enron. Look at CALPERS. Look at Lennar. Two of the three CEO's of these organizations are either in jail, or on the way.

It is clear that Lennar is now a kleptoparasitic organization that preys on all who come within reach. And they are an equal opportunity company: they have defrauded and/or extorted partners, lenders, pensioners, investors, taxpayers, contractors, subcontractors, homebuyers, and have engaged in a wholesale subversion of our legal system to perpetuate their ability to keep doing business the Lennar Way.

The personal costs to me of Lennar's vendetta have been very high: incalculable reputational damage and character assassination, loss of cash and valuable assets, loss of current and future revenues, and the ability to live on a day to day basis in peace. They have routinely hired operatives to beat on our doors at all hours, and we have justifiable fears for our own safety. We have been under surveillance. My phone has been hacked, and private and privileged information has been illegally obtained. Their legal vendetta and thuggish behavior continued night and day and coast to coast.

What is at the bottom of all this? Does it make any sense

for Lennar to expend well over $100,000,000 in corporate resources over simple accounting claims and enforcement of written agreements? Of course not. The only reasonable conclusion one can reach is that there is much more at stake here than meets the eye.

As mentioned earlier, a remarkable book entitled *Tangled Webs: How False Statements Are Undermining America* by Pulitzer-prize winning author, James B. Stewart, explores what he terms a crisis in America: perjury, and false statements occurring at the highest level of business, politics, sports, and culture. And that is certainly the case here. Among his conclusions is that the ultimate responsibility for lying remains with the liar. No excuses.

Another ironic fact is that the Sarbanes Oxley Act (the act that deterred Mr. Miller from signing false reports to the SEC regarding "damage" to Lennar) came about primarily as a direct result of the criminal actions of Mr. Petrocelli's Enron Corporation criminal client, Jeffrey Skilling. Small World.

Lennar plasters variations of the "We Have Integrity" theme on stationary, business cards, websites, advertising, and mirrors. Stuart Miller released a statement to the media that the Miami billion dollar verdict got Lennar's "integrity back."

So, it took a non-stop multi-year effort by Lennar's lawyers culminating in a verdict in Miami obtained by overtly misleading and lying to jurors, using a fraud-on-the-court expert witness, and filing false and unsupportable claims to "get their integrity back?" Well guess what: you can't buy or lie your way into having "integrity."

Another notable fact relevant to this story of colossal

abuse of legal process is that there are profound procedural differences between a superior or circuit court legal process and an appellate legal process. A lower court proceeding is tailor-made for the procedural abuses employed by lawyers like Petrocelli, including but not limited to resource exhaustion and overwhelming or co-opting the typical lower court judges.

An appellate process is different. No discovery, no depositions, no motions, no way to abuse the process. Instead, the rules specify the filing of an appellate brief by an appellant, followed by an answer filed by the appellee, and a final reply by the appellant. That's it. And there are enforced page limits. No ability to engage in a resource exhaustion process.

But there is more: no appellee or appellant knows which judges are assigned to an appeal until the proceeding is almost over.

Lennar and its lawyers have obtained Where-Do-I-Sign punitive orders from friendly circuit and superior court judges along the way. But on their only trip up to an appellate court, in regards to the Lakes "deal-steal" case, a scathing reversal of a superior court decision by the appellate court included this language: *"Lennar manipulated . . . secretly negotiated . . . excluded . . . squeeze out . . . usurp . . . misled."* Draw your own conclusion.

The Lennar executives continue to reap the benefits derived from their odorous business practices while leaving a trail of financial destruction, broken promises, ruined lives in their wake.

It is time Lennar and its executives become accountable

for their actions. Who knows? Maybe someone or some organization will take note and rescind their get-out-of-jail-free cards. The restitution and fines alone would make it worthwhile to bring these bad actors to justice. At minimum, the public should be protected from these predators.

The response to this book will no doubt be more out of the same well-worn playbook. Denial. Diversion. Name calling. Labeling. Lawsuits. Media spin. All will be posted on this book's website as it occurs. So, let the spin begin.

That is the real Lennar story. If you are considering doing business with them, let my experience and this book be your guide and inform your decision. Proceed at your peril.

SHARE YOUR LENNAR STORY / CONTACT US

To view any of the documents cited in this book, or to view more information regarding Lennar and their practices, please visit www.billiondollarlies.com.

It is probable that this book will be followed by an indepth documentary on Lennar, and if you would like to share in confidence your story about your experiences with Lennar or with its lawyers, you can write us at:

Swan Mountain Press
1745 Broadway, 17th Floor
NY, NY 10019
Attn: Billion Dollar Lies

or email us at info@swanmountainpress.com.

TIMELINE

August 5, 1995 — 1st meeting with Lennar Vice President Jon Jaffe in San Francisco.

August 27, 1997 — Sign operating agreement with Lennar to develop Bridges at Rancho Santa Fe. London & Associates Business Plan adopted by operating company, HCC.

Late August 1997 — Lennar CEO Leonard Miller, Founder of Lennar, steps down. Stuart Miller appointed CEO.

January 15, 1998 — Chasman Letter proposing Lennar's best and brightest as candidates to manage Bridges development on a daily basis.

February 1, 1998 — Lennar becomes Bridges development company manager.

February 1, 1998 — Commence development of Bridges at Rancho Santa Fe.

June 25, 1999 — Marsch wires $37,500,000 as a capital contribution to Bridges operating company, HCC.

June 25, 1999 — Lennar secretly transfers the entire $37,500,000 capital contribution to their own accounts.

June 1999 — Bridges operating company commences sale of real estate and memberships. Real estate sales prices substantially exceed projected prices. Membership prices also exceed projected pricing.

June 1999 — Lennar issues first monthly management report for Bridges operating company.

June 1999 — Marsch retained a forensic accounting specialist to review first monthly management report after finding large discrepancies in accounting and cash handling procedures by Lennar.

August 2002 — Lennar and Marsch sign a statutory tolling agreement after Lennar fails to provide accounting numbers.

February 2006 — Lennar secretly transfers a Bridges development company opportunity, the Lakes, to themselves and a friend of Stuart Miller.

September 2006 — Problems related to subprime mortgages and other factors signal a sharp downturn in home-building and mortgage markets.

November 2006 — Lennar swindles predecessor of FDIC using inflated appraisals and straw buyers in Ft. Myers, Florida.

November 3, 2006 — Jaffe communication to Marsch re Lennar inability to provide Bridges accounting numbers, citing "housing market in absolute freefall."

November 13, 2006 — Jaffe communication to Marsch re Lennar inability to provide Bridges accounting numbers, citing "Chairman passed away."

November 13, 2006 — Lawsuit filed regarding Lakes deal steal

December 22, 2006 — Lawsuit filed regarding Bridges accounting and conversion.

January 2007 — A full scale market collapse related to homebuilding and mortgage markets gets underway

February 2, 2007 — Lennar buys out the Quadrant Lakes interest at above market price, shifting significant losses to Lennar shareholders.

February 2007 — Lennar retains Daniel Petrocelli to defend misappropriation claims, and commences a "scorch-earth" litigation campaign.

March 1, 2007 — Lennar swindles CALPERS and a Barclays Bank loan syndicate for $1,400,000,000 then Lennar and LNR pay a 1.4 billion dollar special dividend to themselves from LandSource LLC.

April 3, 2007 — A Lennar internal communication details looting of Lennar-controlled entities to prop up LandSource.

September 27, 2007 — Jon Jaffe acquires $5,000,000 secured "loan" from Gulfstream Finance and Canyon Capital.

June 8, 2008 — Lennar files bankruptcy on behalf of Land-Source LLC.

July 11, 2008 — Letter to Lennar Board citing Lennar accounting issues, requesting an investigation.

September 19, 2008 — Lennar files complaint in Miami re letter to Board.

October 30, 2008 — An anonymous whistleblower mails a letter to Marsch detailing Lennar accounting abuses and criminal behavior.

November 21, 2008 — Lennar stock price is $3.64

January 8, 2009 — J.P. Morgan issues a report calling for lower price for Lennar stock.

January 9, 2009 — FDI publishes a Red Flags Report regarding Lennar.

January 9, 2009 — Stuart Miller appears on CNBC.

January 12, 2009 — Lennar issues a press release denouncing the FDI report.

January 13, 2009 — Regularly scheduled Lennar Board meeting.

April 9, 2010 — Jaffe's lender named in Orange County in a $140,000,000 money laundering complaint.

June 8, 2010 — Complaint filed on behalf of LandSource LLC unsecured creditors detailing massive fraud by Lennar on CALPERS and Barclays Bank using inflated appraisals and fabricated cash flows.

March 15, 2011 — Petrocelli letter to United States Attorney's office in Miami.

May 2, 2011 — Petrocelli letter to United States Attorney's office in Miami.

February 29, 2012 — Orders issued by Cayman Islands High Court re Jaffe's Mortgage Lender in a $140,000,000 money-laundering case.

August 21, 2013 — FDIC sues Lennar for fraud, fraud in the inducement, citing false appraisals and straw buyers over Ft. Myers, FL real estate swindle.

December 2, 2013 — Miami trial.

ABOUT THE AUTHOR

Nicolas Marsch is a commercial and residential real estate developer and investor. He also served in the U.S. Navy and worked primarily in the area of highly classified ship-born radar and combat systems. His development and investment activities include a portfolio of high-end, mixed-use properties composed of ski resort properties, retail centers, ocean-front residences, and mixed use residential and recreational communities. He is the founding developer of the Bridges at Rancho Santa Fe, a world-class golf and residential community in San Diego, CA. He also served on the unsecured creditors committee of Land-Source LLC, a major topic of this book, and was afforded a unique opportunity to peer inside and observe the unscrupulous business practices of one of the nation's largest homebuilders, the Lennar Corporation.

NOTES AND SOURCES

This book has been written primarily using court transcripts, depositions taken under oath, documents obtained in the litigation process, observations of the conduct of the Lennar executives and their lawyers by myself and others, complaints filed in numerous venues across the country involving Lennar, news articles, analyst reports, SEC filings, published reports, press releases, communications to U.S. Attorneys by Lennar lawyers, expert opinions, and other sources. Documents and references are listed by chapter, and chapters containing no referenced documents are purposefully omitted for brevity and clarity. To view the documents referenced in this book, please visit our website: www.billiondollarlies.com.

INTRODUCTION

epidemic of lying: James B. Stewart, *Tangled Webs* (The Penguin Press, 2011).

CHAPTER ONE: An Interesting Day

Fraud Discovery Institute: Red Flags Report, January 9, 2009.

Stuart Miller with Diane Olick: *CNBC* transcript, January 9, 2009.

Lennar Corporation: press release, January 12, 2009.

J.P. Morgan: analyst report, January 8, 2009.

Lennar Corporation stock prices analysis: November 2008 – November 2009

CHAPTER TWO: The Lennar Way

extremely vulnerable: Lennar Corporation and Lennar Homes of California v. Briarwood Capital, Nicolas Marsch et al: 11th Circuit Court District, Miami-Dade County, Florida: transcript of proceedings, December 2, 2013.

Lennar accused of fraud: Dick Hogan, Ft. Myers News-Press, August 21, 2013.

Lennar Corporation et al vs. Briarwood Capital LLC and Nicolas Marsch, Miami-Dade County, Florida: complaint, November 19, 2008.

CHAPTER FOUR: The Beginning

The Bridges Development: www.thebridgesrsf.com.

The London Group Realty Advisors Inc: business plan: July 16, 1997.

Bank of America: corporate deposit statement: June 25, 1999.

We all lost: Stuart Miller with Diane Olick: CNBC transcript, January 9, 2009.

Very profitable: Stuart Miller: certified deposition transcript, May 23, 2012.

Just to be clear: Jon Jaffe: certified trial transcript, September 9, 2009.

The Bridges did fabulously well: Gary London: certified trial transcript, August 10, 2009.

Purpose…"to make money": Jon Jaffe: certified trial transcript, August 31, 2009.

Project been profitable? "No, it has not": Jon Jaffe: certified deposition transcript, June 1, 2012.

The Bridges development lost money every year: Jon Jaffe: certified deposition transcript, August 13, 2012.

Anonymous: whistle blower letter, October 30, 2008.

plow horse: Jon Jaffe: certified trial transcript, September 9, 2009.

CHAPTER FIVE: The Best and Brightest

The best and brightest: Marc Chasman: Memorandum Re: G & A expenses, January 15, 1998.

I want to again apologize: Jon Jaffe: email, November 21, 2006.

Jon Jaffe: certified trial transcript: March 24, 2010.

CHAPTER SIX: A Masters in Mendacity

Helicopter: Jon Jaffe: certified deposition transcript, January 23, 2007.

Under oath: *Jon Jaffe*: certified deposition transcript, January 23, 2007.

Marsch treated Lennar with integrity: *Jon Jaffe:* certified deposition transcript, January 24, 2007.

Not true: *Jon Jaffe:* certified deposition transcript, June 1, 2012.

Witness coaching: Jon Jaffe: certified trial transcript, September 9, 2009.

CHAPTER SEVEN: Flim Flam Accounting

Big Big mistake: Marc Chasman: email, November 7, 2006.

Doug Anderson: certified trial transcript, July 6, 2009

CHAPTER EIGHT: LandSource

Key decision maker: Jon Jaffe: certified deposition transcript, January 23, 2007.

LandSource Creditor Litigation Liquidating Trust v. LNR NWHL Holdings, LNR Land Partners, and LNR Property Corporation, Delaware Bankruptcy Court: complaint, June 8, 2011.

We try to do things strategically and by plan: Stuart Miller: certified deposition transcript, September 16, 2008.

The housing market is in just absolute freefall: Jon Jaffe: email, November 3, 2006.

Wrong and inappropriate: Mike White: certified trial transcript, March 10, 2010.

Ouch!!!: Chrissy Parker: memo, April 3, 2007.

Summary of quarterly cash balances of Lennar Corporation for 10Q filings: 2006 and 2007.

Stuart Miller with Diane Olick: CNBC transcript, January 9, 2009.

Dale Kasler: *The Sacramento Bee*, August 3, 2010

Dire straits: Tyler Durden: *Zero Hedge*, May 18, 2010.

United States of America v. Federico R. Buenrostro, Jr: plea agreement, July 11, 2014.

CHAPTER NINE: Litigation Vendetta

In excess of $50,000,000: Stuart Miller: certified deposition transcript, May 23, 2012.

Under $50 or $100,000: Stuart Miller: certified deposition transcript, May 24, 2012.

CHAPTER TEN: The Whistleblower Letter

Anonymous: whistleblower letter, October 30, 2008.

Fraud Discovery Institute: Red Flags Report, January 9, 2009.

Whistleblower testimony:

Stuart Miller: certified deposition testimony, May 24, 2012.

Mark Sustana: certified deposition testimony, August 1, 2012.

Jon Jaffe: certified deposition testimony, August 13, 2012.

CHAPTER ELEVEN: Fraud Discovery Institute

Sincere thanks: U.S. Department of Justice, Federal Bureau of Investigations: letter, September 9, 1996.

I cannot thank you enough: City National Bank: letter, January 21, 2003.

Your participation was invaluable: U.S. Department of Justice, Federal Bureau of Investigations: letter, March 8, 2004.

Extremely well done: Department of the Army: letter, April 17, 1998.

Impressive, engaging and insightful: O'Melveny & Myers LLP: letter, July 22, 2002.

Fraud Discovery Institute: engagement letter, November 30, 2008.

CHAPTER TWELVE: The Red Flags Report

Fraud Discovery Institute: Red Flags Report, January 9, 2009.

J.P. Morgan: analyst report, January 8, 2009.

Daniel Petrocelli: letter to U.S. Attorney's Office, March 15, 2011.

Daniel Petrocelli: letter to U.S. Attorney's Office, May 2, 2011.

Jon Jaffe: Secured $5,000,000 Promissory Note.

Jon Jaffe: AFX Property Report, June 4, 2012.

Lennar Corporation: press release, January 12, 2009.

Jon Jaffe: certified deposition transcript, August 13, 2012.

Gray1 CPB LLC v. Gulfstream Finance Inc. et al, County of Orange: complaint, April 9, 2010.

Grand Court of the Cayman Islands, Financial Services Division: request for international judicial assistance, January 24, 2012.

I believe that to be a correct statement: Stuart Miller: certified deposition transcript, May 23, 2012.

Mike White: certified trial transcript, March 10, 2010.

Ouch!!!: Chrissy Parker: internal Lennar memo, April 3, 2007.

Anonymous: whistleblower letter, October 30, 2008.

Stuart Miller with Diane Olick: CNBC transcript, January 9, 2009.

Equity positions, in some instances, had been wiped out: Stuart Miller: certified deposition transcript, May 23, 2012.

Teresa Burney: *Builder Magazine online*, February 4, 2009.

Lennar Corporation: 10Q SEC Report, May 31, 2009.

Ponzi scheme: Irving Bolotin: certified deposition transcript, February 17, 2010.

Ponzi scheme: Bruce Gross: certified trial testimony, December 2, 2013.

CHAPTER THIRTEEN: Kill the Messengers

Briarwood Capital LLC: letter to Lennar Board of Directors, July 11, 2008.

Lennar Corporation et al v. Briarwood Capital LLC and Nicolas Marsch, Miami-Dade county: complaint, November 19, 2008.

Lennar Corporation: press release, January 12, 2009.

Fraud Discovery Institute: Red Flags Report, January 9, 2009.

Anonymous: whistleblower letter, October 30, 2008.

Daniel Petrocelli: letter to U.S. Attorney's Office, March 15, 2011.

Daniel Petrocelli: letter to U.S. Attorney's Office, May 2, 2011.

Damages and SEC reporting. Stuart Miller: certified deposition transcript, August 7, 2012.

Lennar Corporation: 10Q SEC report, February 28, 2009.

In-person meetings: Stuart Miller: certified deposition transcript, May 24, 2012.

I don't recall: Stuart Miller: certified deposition transcript, August 7, 2012.

Board of Directors of Lennar Corporation: meeting minutes, January 13, 2009.

Harvey A. Silverglate, *Three Felonies a Day* (Encounter Books, 2009)

CHAPTER FOURTEEN: The Board of Mushrooms

I don't know: Kirk Landon: certified deposition transcript, February 17, 2010.

Irving Bolotin: certified deposition transcript, February 17, 2010.

Fraud Discovery Institute: Red Flags Report, January 9, 2009.

Board of Directors of Lennar Corporation: meeting minutes, January 13, 2009.

CHAPTER FIFTEEN: The Deal Steal

I think that's a fair characterization: Jon Jaffe: certified deposition transcript, January 23, 2007.

Try to grow the relationship: Jon Jaffe: certified deposition transcript, January 25, 2007.

Anonymous: whistle blower letter, October 30, 2008.

Briarwood Capital LLC v. Lennar Homes of California et al, Court of Appeal, Fourth Appellate District: Lakes appellate opinion, December 1, 2010.

Pursuing a strategy: Mike Levesque: Quadrant Membership Interest Purchase, February 9, 2007.

Quadrant Investment Group: webpage: Portfolio, January 2007.

Double date: Stuart Miller: certified deposition transcript, September 12, 2008.

Lakes Mediation Brief, October 26, 2007.

Things haven't worked out well: Jon Jaffe: certified deposition transcript, January 25, 2007.

CHAPTER SIXTEEN: The Florida Billion Dollar Verdict

Theodore J. Boutrous, Jr., "Big Legal Battles, Bigger Lies", *USA Today*, April 16, 2014.

Paul M. Barrett, *Law of the Jungle* (Crown Publishers 2014).

Lennar Corporation and Lennar Homes of California v. Briarwood Capital, Nicolas Marsch, et al: 11th Circuit Court District, Miami-Dade County: transcript of proceedings, December 2, 2013.

CHAPTER SEVENTEEN: Frivolous Claims and The Florida Fairy Tale

Briarwood Capital LLC: letter to Lennar Board of Directors, July 11, 2008.

I think he had the right to send a letter, and I read it: Irving Bolotin: certified deposition transcript, February 17, 2010.

Scott Cooper: declaration, September 17, 2012.

John E. Jorgensen, The Sylint Group: Computer Forensic Expert Report, November 12, 2012.

"Facts do not exist. Facts are created": Paul M. Barrett, *Law of the Jungle* (Crown Publishers 2014).

.

CHAPTER EIGHTEEN: A Liar for Hire

"lawyer's duty of candor": James B. Stewart, *Tangled Webs* (The Penguin Press 2011).

.

CHAPTER NINETEEN: RICO: The Lennar Way

Contractor Extortion:

Roger Showley, "Lennar asks contractors for discounts on finished work," *The San Diego Union-Tribune,* March 2, 2007.

Robert P. Mader, "Builder tells subs to cut prices mid-contract," *Contractor Magazine*, March 1, 2007.

Beth Curran, "National Builder Reneges on Contracts, Threatens Trades," *California Professional Association of Specialty Contractors*, February 27, 2007.

Paradise Palms, LLC v. Len Paradise, LLC, et al: complaint, December 16, 2009.

Cellular Phone Hacking. Ben Levitan: expert's declaration, June 20, 2012.

Jon Jaffe: certified deposition transcript, August 13, 2012.

CHAPTER TWENTY: Just the Facts

Fraud Discovery Institute: Red Flags Report, January 9, 2009.

James B. Stewart, *Tangled Webs* (The Penguin Press 2011).

CPSIA information can be obtained at www.ICGtesting.com
Printed in the USA
BVOW05*1403080215

386612BV00001B/1/P